EARL SCRUGGS

AND THE

5-STRING BANJO

Illustrated by
Burt Brent, M.D.

PEER INTERNATIONAL CORPORATION

1619 BROADWAY • NEW YORK, N. Y. 10019

Dedicated to

My Wife And Children

T.T Bledsoe '70

Acknowledgments

I would like to express my appreciation to Billy Keith and Burt Brent for the assistance they gave me in preparing this book.

I first met Billy in 1962 when our show was appearing in concert at John Hopkins University. Billy came back stage after the concert and he had a notebook with him that contained tablature to all of my songs. We discussed the idea of Billy coming to Nashville to work with me on the book, which resulted in his spending several weeks with me working on the tablature.

I met Burt in the fall of 1964 when he was serving at the Ft. Campbell Army Base, in Kentucky. We spent an average of three nights each week for approximately six months working on the text of the book. I would play the rolls and the left hand exercises and Burt would write them down. I would also like to express my thanks to him for the illustrations and a number of photographs that are used throughout this book and the cover photograph of Stevie Scruggs and myself.

Earl Scruggs

The author would also like to express his appreciation to the following. . . .

Grandpa Jones, Stringbean, Dorris Macon, Thomas B. Allen, Radio Station WSM, and "Snuffy" DeWitt Jenkins, for photographs.

Warren Kennison, Jr. for his assistance in preparing parts of the tablature.

"Shot" Jackson for his contribution on banjo finishing.

Golden West Melodies, Inc. and Gene Autry for permission to reprint "Blue Ridge Cabin Home" and "Shuckin' The Corn".

Carolintone Music Co., Inc.; Chappel & Co., Ltd.; J. Albert & Son Music Publishers and Paul Henning for permission to reprint "The Ballad Of Jed Clampett".

Martha White Mills, Inc. for permission to reprint "You Bake Right With Martha White" (The Martha White Theme).

Pamper Music, Inc. for permission to reprint "Hot Corn, Cold Corn".

Flatt & Scruggs Publishing Co., Inc. for permission to reprint "Nashville Blues".

EARL SCRUGGS
AND THE 5 STRING BANJO

TABLE OF CONTENTS

Foreword

by NAT WINSTON, M.D.

There's a classic success story known to everyone in the world of music. This is the tale of the cheap, third-rate musical instrument, long discarded because its sounds were tinny and rasping to the ear, until one day, in the hands of a master, it poured forth notes as golden as the melodies which are said to fill celestial spheres. This vignette, even with its sob element, rests upon a truth so basic that it approaches the status of legend.

We all give clues to ourselves: our choice of clothing, our way of entering a room, our approach to a musical instrument. We've met persons who at the moment of introduction cast a spell over us. Their whole manner advertises an inner brightness, intelligence, a warm capacity for friendship. So we make it our business to know them better, only to find, when we do, that they are like a picturesque river which hides in its waters unexpected shallows and sharp rocks. The shallowness and sharpness of a human being's character can be camouflaged by an overwhelming personality.

Our personalities, although structured fundamentally alike, vary according to our individual environments and our separate ways of resolving inner conflicts. Different settings and emotional habits produce different patterns of personality as definitely as different dies produce different forms of engravings. For example, the Oriental concept of beauty, both in sight and sound, frequently sets Occidental nerves on edge as we listen to the half-notes and quarter-notes of the scales that to them are melodious, but to us are devoid of musical meaning.

Each person can be classified into one of about fifteen personality types. The type of defense mechanisms we use most naturally and consistently gives the name to our pattern, for these mechanisms make up our approach to life. Some persons, for instance, apparently feel at home in any group of people, they size up any situation and handle it appropriately. This can be a natural thing or it can be a protective facade, consciously or almost unconsciously donned to cover an inside insecurity. Other individuals, equally sensitive to others, no less acutely tuned in on the atmosphere around them, are much less comfortable about their ability to cope. The latter person, highly intelligent, perhaps vulnerably sensitive, may naturally turn to a non-human object to relate to. A classic illustration is the esteemed professor, self-consciously devoid of small talk at a party but brilliantly at ease while he's at work on a mathematical formula or a physics problem . . . the latter circumstances make no direct demands that he relate to other people. Conversely, of course, the man who converses easily among his fellows can probably never reach the professor's skill in a physical science, for his energies are channeled in other directions.

So it is with musicians. Men of artistic genius, who combine talent and human sensitivity with an inability or reluctance to relate directly to other human beings, can most fulfillingly relate to an instrument; and this instrument becomes, for them, the vehicle through which they liberate their thoughts and feelings. Inaccurately and unfairly, it can bring upon their heads the charge of aloofness. All too often, the artist is pictured as a rather distant being, cold and oblivious to human feelings. He is none of these things. If the musician were emotionally removed from the rest of humanity, he would not be able to express in his music all of the poignancy that this humanity has ever felt. In common with the rest of us, he has his flaws and foibles, but cold he is not. In all of the music that is his communication, warmth comes through as clearly as his talent.

Another person might direct his primary energies and emotions into other fields and directions, and therefore would not have sufficient energy or personality resources "left over" to put into the mastery of music, whatever his store of natural talent for it might be. The musician is what he is because not merely his natural talent — however abundant — but his energy and personality are channeled in this one direction. His feelings are expressed by music and by his deeply personal choice of a musical instrument.

The mediocrity of a musical instrument can go unnoticed when it's manipulated by a genius, for his handling of it and the sounds he draws from it will contain nothing of mediocrity. For that while, the instrument will speak the musician's quality, and not its own. The artist's style is as distinctive as his handwriting. His style is, in fact, his signature.

Those of us who expose ourselves to music at every opportunity become easily familiar with the characteristic techniques of the different symphony orchestra conductors, country music artists, leaders of the dance bands. During World II, when the big-name bands held musical sway over the whole country, none of us needed the interruption of the radio announcer to tell us whether a record of Frenesi had been cut by Artie Shaw or Tommy Dorsey. We recognized each man's mode, and we recognized that his style came so close to being a philosophy that it permeated the playing of every man under his leadership. We can walk into an auditorium, never having met the musician who is going to perform, and leave after the program feeling that we know him, because we do. He has been interpreting himself to us, through a medium almost as old as human speech.

We even know, however musically uninitiated we may be, whether an instrumental number we hear on the jukebox was played by male or female. The masculine touch differs. For that matter, we tend to assign sexual properties to the instruments themselves, much as French or Spanish linguists assign the masculine or feminine gender to every noun in their vocabulary. The harp and guitar we think of as feminine, the bass tuba masculine (where is the female who could even begin to hoist that latter object?). The five-string banjo has, so far as it's known throughout its history, been a man's way to music. It's a rare woman who has known this instrument understandingly enough to become a virtuoso.

With such clearcut variations existing in our concepts of the musical instrument, it follows naturally that certain personalities are drawn almost without their own volition to certain types of instruments, and even that it takes a certain personality type to be able to make music his individual means of expression with **any** instrument, even granting that native talent is his to be expressed.

Personality alone does not make for bona fide artistry. There is also the element of talent. To the best of our knowledge, talent is an inborn potentiality which can be developed into skill. Inborn ability is an inherited situation of the multiple genes theory. According to Mendelian inheritance laws, the parents of four children have half-genes for music and half non-genes for music, in which event two of the children might take to music as naturally as to breathing air, while the other two could live out their lives as musical duds. Talent, then, makes for the opportunity to practice and become an artist. However, many talents go to waste because of lack of will to utilize or develop them. At the same time, many of us, though lacking a great talent, thoroughly enjoy an instrument, love its music, and can go on to study, practice, and enjoy the beauties and relaxation that it can provide.

Until Earl Scruggs' nation wide debut on the Grand Ole Opry in 1945, banjo players were traditionally a rowdy lot, were comedians of a sort, and most often didn't take their banjo playing seriously. Played mainly by extroverts, whose handling of a tune was to throw it at you, the banjo itself had become the extrovert of musical instruments. It was strictly for fun, nothing to be taken seriously, nothing to be thought about, and certainly nothing to be loved except with the "rough-'em-up" form of affection you might bestow on a friendly pup. Even the four-string, or tenor banjo was only for loud strumming while square-dancers pounded their feet to a coarse rhythm or while crowds whooped it up in a noisy honky-tonk. The nearest any banjo came to being admitted to polite society was its times of being permitted, always as a single piece, in an orchestra, at which times it had to be "toned down" in order to blend in with the more respectable instruments. In the Southern Applachians, no decent woman would let her husband associate with a banjo player and certainly no father would see that fate befall his innocent daughter. The habitat of the banjo was the moonshine still. My father, who loved this instrument despite its reputation, wrote this poem in connection with the prevailing attitude:

Ode To A Banjo

Nat T. Winston, Sr.
1918

Alas! My banjo, thou art broken,
I quietly lay thee down to rest
Accept these lines, an humble token
From one who deems that thou hast blest.

I know hard things were said of thee—
My once vivacious friend;
And those who hate high revelry,
Rejoice at thine end.

But, still to me a friend thou wert,
For with thy cheerful song;
Ye could the darkest hours convert,
And bid care flee along.

For they were songs I understood,
Not highclass throbs and moans;
Real human songs, not angel's food,
Were in thy lively tones.

I loved you not for virtures sake,
For naught of her ye knew;
Ye ever were a shameless rake,
And yet I loved ye true.

I loved you for your very sins,
You merry hearted knave;
I loved you for those wicked dins,
That made the parsons rave!

He wrote this, incidentally, even after having been told by a mountain minister that, "you might as well give your son a ticket to hell as give him a five-string banjo!" This is what can happen to the good name of the most delicate instrument before an artist adopts it for his own.

Fortunately, an artist did. Earl Scruggs restored dignity and the intricate beauty we now enjoy in the five-string banjo, one of music's finest instruments. If I were to settle upon one word to describe Earl, the man and the musician, I might choose "perceptive." As his vast audiences know, Earl doesn't use many words. He doesn't really need them, as he's as finely attuned as any musical instrument. He picks up the nuances of a song or a situation; his acknowledgement of them, and his reply, in his music. Like his approach to the world around him, Earl's approach to a musical passage can have a complexity of shading. The sensitivity of the artist shows in the sensitive overtones and undercurrents of his interpretations. After many years of personal friendship with Earl, I can notice times in our conversation when our words are playing second fiddle to his mental involvement with a new pattern of sound. He may be talking to me about yesterday's weather, but his thoughts are on tomorrow's modification of a particular lick on the banjo.

The five-string banjo has become almost synonymous with the genius of the first man who gave it its rightful place, and who continues through his relationship with it to earn his title of "The World's Most Imitated Musician," and the style is now known throughout the world as "Scruggs-Style Banjo Picking."

To be sure, the five-string banjo is still for fun, but consists of a new type of fun, intricacy and beauty in its melodies, rather than slambang roughness. Like a complete person, like the person who plays it, its approach to life is not limited to one mood. It can rolic with joy; but it can also mourn. It can speak of love or hate, show tenderness or anger. And, it can sound a wistfulness that words have not captured. This is the five-string banjo today, yours to enjoy.

The History And Development Of America's Favorite Folk Instrument

by **LOUISE SCRUGGS**

No sound is more deeply rooted in American history than the thrilling ring of the five-string banjo. Our national instrument, seventy-five or a hundred years ago, was played by many thousands of people, and yet, by 1940, the instrument and the secrets of playing it had almost died. Modern Americans had almost forgotten the friendly ring of that fifth string until a group of young enthusiasts refused to let it die and once again began "strumming on the old banjo."

Today, the picture shines with new brilliance, and the old-time banjo and the wonderful music once played on it are enjoying a new vogue. This American folk art was saved principally through the unreconstructed stubborness of certain musicians in the Appalachian Mountains and the Carolinas who simply paid no attention when they were told the banjo was dead.

The banjo has an amazing history to match its sparkling sound. The ancient ancestor of the banjo, an instrument called the Rebec, originated in Arabia a thousand years ago and can still be purchased today in the larger marts of the Middle East. It consists of a skin head stretched over a gourd or hollow body with a neck holding three gut strings. The Rebec was probably carried both east and west with the spread of Islam.

Negro slaves brought it to the United States from North and West Africa. In his "Notes on the State of Virginia," published in 1785, Thomas Jefferson says the "banjar" was the principal musical instrument of the American Negroes. By this time, the banjo had developed into a four-stringed instrument. But the true American Banjo was not invented until 1831, when a banjo enthusiast named Joel Sweeney made a small but revolutionary modification. He added a fifth string, higher in pitch than any of the others, right next to the lowest pitched string, and secured by a peg mounted halfway up the neck.

There has been some discussion as to whether or not the fifth string was added by someone in another country at an earlier date than the Sweeney invention. There were other five stringed instruments before Sweeney's invention, but the strings ran all the way up the neck and were not constructed like the five-string banjos we know today. If the fifth string was added somewhere else, to our knowledge it was done independently, while Joel Sweeney added his fifth string in 1831, oblivious to any existing similar instrument, and thus provided America with the instrument that she enjoys today and knows as her national instrument. This odd instrument, with four pegs at the top of the neck and one peg sticking out on the side, captured the heart of America and is known as America's most original and distinctive musical invention.

Joel Walker Sweeney
Photo: Courtesy of the History Division of the Los Angeles County Museum

Joel Sweeney was born in Appomattox, Virginia in 1813. At an early age, Sweeney organized his own Appomattox band. He composed many songs based on the melodies created by the slaves he knew and loved. Billed as the "Banjo King," he was a hit on the New York stage after a wagon tour through the South. His fame carried him to England, where he appeared before Queen Victoria at a command performance. Research has disclosed that what is believed to be "America's first banjo" is now in the possession of the Los Angeles County Museum in California.

Photos of the Sweeney banjo.

Courtesy of the History Division of the Los Angeles County Museum.

During his lifetime, Joel was the foremost of the blackface minstrels, and has been called the "father of American minstrelsy." It has been said that his company was the first of a long line of minstrel shows which continued as popular entertainment up until the 1890's.

The fifth string is the blend in the banjo and creates the familiar ring, being plucked solely by the thumb. No other instrument in the world was strung like the five-string banjo, and entirely new playing methods were developed that are unique to the instrument. Thousands of nameless Americans developed these playing methods during long evenings in log cabins, shoddy shanties, river steamships, and gold-mining boom towns. The banjo went west in covered wagons and was enjoyed by both whites and Negroes throughout the nation.

No two people had exactly the same method for working in that fifth string. For that matter, many people used four or five different tunings and changed both the tunings and the style to play different songs. Little music has ever been written for the banjo. Instead, a tremendous amount of lore developed and was passed on from player to player; old folks taught the young ones, and good players swapped style secrets. In a nation of rugged individualists, the banjo was an appropriately individualistic instrument. Banjoists played "old time songs" now called folk music. The popularity of the banjo was important in perpetuating and preserving many songs that otherwise would have been forgotten. In addition, a special body of "banjo music" began to develop, and this too, is now part of America's folk music heritage. For the most part, the authors of this music are virtually unknown, as are the early inventors of the principal playing styles.

Throughout the nineteenth century, the banjo held its place in America's affections, but around the turn of the century a decline set in. The advent of jazz was one factor in this decline, in that jazz musicians altered the banjo and the method of playing it in order to adapt it to the new jazz combos. Joel Sweeney's fifth string was dropped, completely killing the distinctiveness of the instrument. The neck was shortened, the head enlarged, and heavier strings were used. The resulting four-string, or tenor banjo, was installed in jazz bands and was strummed, the old finger-picking styles being abandoned along with the fifth string. The banjo was expected to produce enough volume to be heard through a brass section. In some cases, the change went even further and the instrument was reduced to mandolin size and strung with eight strings. Such instruments did not sound even remotely like the old-time banjo. These innovations apparently signalled the death knell of the five-string banjo and only a few bands and natives of the more remote recesses of the South kept the old tradition going.

In the 1920's, when commercial recording companies put out their earliest folk discs, some of the remaining old-time banjo players were recorded. These records, once looked upon as beneath the notice of "cultured" people, are now among our most important sources of American Folk music. Before country or folk music became highly commercial, these performers played true folk songs in their own native style. Most of the master discs were destroyed but the records that survived are now rare, precious, and sometimes very costly collectors' items. Perhaps, most important of all, the scraps and fragments of the old playing styles, the songs, and the pure authentic sound of the banjo have now been preserved on long playing records. Several recording companies sent teams with tape recorders into the remote recesses of the South and have issued records of some of the old-timers who are still living. (There is an album titled, "American Banjo—Songs And Tunes In Scruggs Style," illustrating some of the older generation's playing and some younger performers, playing in a three-finger style.)

By 1930, the four-string banjo was fading out. It was rarely used in jazz or popular music bands. As for the five-string instrument, fewer and fewer people remembered how to play it. America was on the verge of losing one of its most remarkable folk arts. During these lean years, a few performers stuck stubbornly by their five-string banjos, certain players in bands in the Southern mountains, and a few performers on country music radio shows such as the famous WSM's Grand Ole Opry.

Yet, by 1940, even the country music bands were dropping the five-string banjo. The banjo players who remained playing on radio were usually billed as a single attraction and not included in a group of musicians. By this time, the instrument was no longer being made except on special order and the demand was very limited. A few folklorists began discovering the five-string banjo and recognized it as one of our most remarkable contributions to the world's music. It was soon after World War II that a few bands began using the banjo again.

Earl Scruggs, during this time, had developed a new playing style that was soon being imitated throughout the nation. He introduced what is now known as "Scruggs Style Picking" on the Grand Ole Opry in 1945. His style spread rapidly and within two years, the demand for the five-string banjo was so great that the instrument companies had begun to manufacture them again. This style of playing is heard among many of the country and folk groups today. The bands which now use a banjo in their group are increasing steadily throughout the United States and in foreign countries.

Today, our nation and a great part of the world are aware of the great mass of music that the "folk" have provided and still provide. In the vast Library of Congress in Washington, D.C., there is stored a huge collection of songs preserved in record form. These songs can be heard by lovers of folk music long after the artists who play and sing them are gone.

American universities have sent scholars into neighborhoods where various ethnic groups live in order to understand more fully their folklore and music. Their reports help us to understand all the people who make up our country. Knowledge of a nations folklore is knowledge of the creative working of the minds of its people, and a key to that nations values.

America owes much to the players of the five-string banjo, who held staunch against the tide, and preserved a precious and wonderful heritage when nobody else cared.

*Parts of the preceding article were printed in the following publiactions: © March 1961, Tennessee Folklore Society Bulletin; © 1963-1964 December, January issue SING OUT!

The following personalities are some of the people who perpetuated interest in the banjo. There are many other really fine musicians in the country today who should be given credit, but space does not permit us to include all of them.

Uncle Dave Macon

"Uncle Dave," as he was affectionately known, was a rotund minstrel with gold teeth and a big gold watch chain, whose uninhibited performances on the five-string banjo were one of the Grand Ole Opry's best loved attractions.

Earl Scruggs and Dr. Nat Winston recently visited in the home of Dorris Macon, Uncle Dave's son, and the following information was obtained:

Uncle Dave was born on October 7, 1870, at Smartt Station, Tennessee, in Warren County. His father was a hotel keeper in Nashville who catered to the theatrical profession. Uncle Dave learned to play the banjo by watching performers who stopped at the hotel.

Before he went into show business, he operated a freight line from Murfreesboro to Woodbury, Tennessee. The freight line was a wagon team consisting of two wagons, with three mules to each wagon, one of them being at the end of the tongue in order to help pull the wagons over the hills. Four toll gates were located between Murfreesboro and Woodbury and the fee collected went to help pay to keep the roads rocked. Uncle Dave composed a song "On The Dixie-B Line," which was written about the freight line he operated. While he was still running the freight line he recorded "Bile Them Cabbage Down."

In 1920, he and Uncle Jimmy Thompson, the first fiddler on radio, joined a vaudeville show on the RKO circuit.

Dorris recalls that their first radio was an Atwater Kent and the only one in the community. It had wires which were wrapped around an oatmeal box, and a telephone receiver was used to listen to the radio. Only one person could listen at a time.

Uncle Dave's favorite tunes were "Eleven Cent Cotton And Forty Cent Meat," "Bully Of The Town," "Keep My Skillet Good And Greasy," "Bile Them Cabbage Down," and "How Beautiful Heaven Must Be." He never used a pick when he played the banjo.

He was a born comedian and could handle any kind of situation. Just for an example, on one occasion a heckler from the audience called out to him, "You're the first monkey I ever saw play the banjo." Uncle Dave replied, "Yes, and you're the first ape that ever complimented me."

Uncle Dave was also a great philosopher—for example:

"Reminiscenses of Early Life"

"At my advanced age I realize more keenly the great mental powers of youth, and could I command an audience of the youth of our land today, I would say to them: Learn the beautiful things of life in your early years, from Holy Writ we learn. Remember thy Creator in the days of thy youth.'

When a child of six or less, I remember my sister Bettie reading to me the beautiful story of the Garden of Eden with its "Tree of Life" in the center. I associated the word garden then only with the one-acre plot our father had measured off into four equal sections and placed in the center of it the arborvitate, juniper, and apple tree.

In 1883 my father re-moved to Nashville, Tennessee, and the old home place was left to strangers, but the lessons and impressions made there were never erased from my memory. In the yard, near the garden gate, stood a black haw tree about six inches in diameter, that was always loaded with fruit regardless of the season.

After a space of fifty years I returned to the old home to find the beautiful garden with its trees and flowers in a cornfield, but the black haw tree still stood as a sentinel, seeming to say to me,'I remain to remind you of the Great Beyond where no changes ever come.' Therefore, our knowledge and sentiments of this life accompany our souls into eternity, I believe to be true."

Uncle Dave traveled all over the country, playing and singing wherever there were people to listen to him. In 1926, at the age of fifty-six, he joined the Grand Ole Opry, becoming its first singing star and its biggest single attraction for fifteen years thereafter.

Uncle Dave was married to Mary Richardson; they had seven sons. After a short illness, Uncle Dave died on March 22, 1952. The Country Music Association installed Uncle Dave Macon in The Country Music Hall of Fame on October 21, 1966.

"Uncle" Dave Macon and George D. Hay at Uncle Dave's home near Readyville, Tennessee

George D. Hay, shown in the photo with Uncle Dave, was the originator of the Grand Ole Opry. He joined WSM in Nashville after leaving WLS in Chicago where he originated the National Barn Dance. It was on November 28, 1925 at 8 o'clock, when George D. Hay presented himself as "The Solemn Old Judge," and launched the WSM Barn Dance.

His only artist that night was an 80 year old fiddle player named "Uncle" Jimmy Thompson who said he knew a thousand fiddle tunes. He played an hour that first night and didn't want to stop. The impromptu sixty minute event marked the beginning of what was later to become the Grand Ole Opry. Shortly thereafter, musicians began coming to Nashville to play on the program. In 1927, the WSM Barn Dance took on the more descriptive title of Grand Ole Opry.

In the fall of 1927, at the conclusion of a three hour presentation of the NBC Music Appreciation Hour, conducted by Dr. Walter Damrosch, Judge Hay said, "We have been listening to music taken largely from Grand Opera, but from now on we will present "The Grand Ole Opry." He called on Deford Bailey who performed a country version of his "Pan American Blues" on his harmonica.

Judge Hay was a believer and respector of traditional music. If he was enjoying an artist's performance, he would blow his famous steam-boat whistle. While he was on the Grand Ole Opry, if an artist, or group, seemed to be playing too far out, his famous remark was, "Keep it down to earth, Boys, down to earth."

It is fitting that George D. Hay was elected to the Country Music Hall of Fame on October 21, 1966 alongside of Uncle Dave Macon.

Stringbean

Dave "Stringbean" Akeman was born in Annville, Kentucky. Stringbean was raised on a farm with his four brothers and three sisters. Long before he owned a banjo, he spent many childhood hours picking and practicing on imaginary banjo strings in imitation of his father who was a banjo player.

At the age of thirteen, he and a friend made a banjo and learned to play it. In his youth, he farmed with his father and began playing for country music gatherings.

His musical career began at the age of eighteen. His first radio experience was on Radio Station WLAP in Lexington, Kentucky. He worked for three years with Charley Monroe and his Kentucky Partners in Greensboro, North Carolina. In 1942, he became a member of the Grand Ole Opry.

Stringbean has toured with many entertainers and appeared on NBC network radio programs for twelve years. He was a close friend of Uncle Dave Macon, and Uncle Dave willed "String" one of his banjos.

His easy going manner and rustic humor make him a great favorite with the Nashville entertainers and his many, many fans.

Grandpa Jones

Louis M. (Grandpa) Jones, was born in Niagara, Kentucky. Grandpa calls his style of picking thumb string style, claw hammer, drop thumb, and frailing. His musical experience began at the age of eight with his playing the ukelele. At the age of sixteen, he won an amateur contest and played straight roles, singing ballads and novelty numbers.

In 1936, he changed his role to comedian and Bradley Kincaid gave him the nickname of "Grandpa." In 1937, he formed his act, "Grandpa Jones and His Grandchildren," on Radio Station WWVA in Wheeling, West Virginia.

Grandpa recalls that it was in 1937, when he was appearing along with a number of other artists, including Cousin Emmy, when he became interested in the banjo for the first time. He had played only the guitar on the air since 1929. He recalls that he worried Cousin Emmy trying to get her to teach him to play the banjo, until she said, "O.K. I'll teach you the thumb string lick on the banjo." After a few weeks, he was able to use the banjo on the radio for a few numbers.Later, the banjo became more of his trade mark than the guitar.

He joined the Grand Ole Opry in 1947, then left to work radio stations in Virginia. Later, he entertained troops in the Orient and in Europe.

No article on the development of the five-string banjo would be complete without mentioning Pete Seeger, who has done so much to popularize the instrument among the folk song enthusiasts in the cities.

Pete sent the following message to be included in this book.

"They say there's nothing new under the sun. Tens of thousands of years ago probably some early man first plucked a rhythm on a string and made it louder by crossing it over a drum head. What do you bet?

But the plunky, twangy, rippling tones of today's 5-string banjo is the creation of the country musicians of the Southern states of the U.S.A., and chief among them is Mr. Earl Scruggs. The style of music they created is going to be heard in many lands, wherever people love its bright sound, unlike that of any other musical instrument. 'Round and 'round this old world, ring, ring, the banjo!

I'm sure glad to hear that Earl Scruggs is putting out a book about his kind of banjo picking. There will be millions of people wanting to buy it, and I'm one of 'em."

CHAPTER 2

Getting Acquainted With Your Banjo

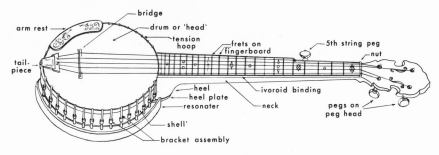

Learn your banjo parts

Where To Get A Banjo:

Depending on how much you want to spend for an instrument, there are several ways of tackling this project. You can either buy a new one from one of the many fine companies that sell them, you might find a used one in a pawn shop, put an ad in a paper, go to an auction, or ask other banjo players if they know of one for sale. Most instrument companies will send you a brochure of their instruments which would probably be very helpful to you in deciding on the brand you would prefer. By this method, you will then have a price list and photos of the different instruments to compare.

If you are left handed, most instrument companies will make a left handed banjo neck on special order.

Hints About Your Banjo And Its Parts:

FINGERBOARD:

A. Your fingerboard should not be warped or badly worn from over use. One way to check for warpage is to lay a straight edge along it, or sight down the neck. More than 1/10 inch bowing will keep your instrument constantly out of pitch, and in most cases, less than 1/10 inch will cause this problem.

B. Smooth sliding action will be noticed if you run a cloth over the fingerboard frequently, and a good finish on the neck will also give you a smoother sliding action. Ebony fingerboards seem to be the smoothest type, as it is a hard wood with a very fine grain. Incidentally, while playing in a performance, I occasionally run the tips of my fingers through my hair to get a sample of hair tonic, then run them across the fingerboard, producing a smoother action.

FRETS:

A. The frets should be rounded in order to slide your fingers up and down the neck smoothly.

B. They may occasionally have to be replaced as the strings tend to groove them after constant use. A simple test is to make sure that the bridge is in the right place first (read the section about the bridge), then play a chromatic scale on each string. (Pluck it open, then fretted at 1st, 2nd, 3rd, etc., all the way up the neck). If two fret positions sound the same note, then one of them is too high or one of them is grooved from constant use.

High frets can be filed down, and grooved frets replaced. I always let a professional instrument repairman do this work on my frets since this is one of the major items. They have a system of "tapping" down high frets but I would not recommend your doing this until you have seen it done and thoroughly understand the correct procedure.

BRACKETS:

Oil the threads each time you change the head to prevent their wearing and stripping. A very thin type oil would be recommended, such as sewing machine oil.

PEGS:

The pegs should turn freely but not slip. They can be adjusted by tightening or loosening the screw that goes through the button . If the screw has a tendency to loosen from retuning, sometimes a very thin washer will correct this. A lock type washer would give better results.

5th STRING PEG:

I use a regular 5th string tuning peg which is gearless. There are two reasons for this; number one, for quick replacement of a string after one has broken during a performance; number two, the uniqueness, and this is only a matter of what you like or dislike.

The real danger to this type of peg, which is only pressed into the hole, is that it will easily wear the hole large and will no longer hold if life-long care is not given it. I have corrected worn necks with plastic wood. A good practice is to loosen the set screw while changing the string. In more than twenty years of professional playing and daily use, I haven't stripped one through this method. You will also want to keep it clean inside.

There are some very attractive non-geared pegs being made. Also, geared pegs which help in tuning when the string is to be moved a very slight amount.

For best service, keep the screw set with only enough tension to keep the string from slipping while you are playing.

In many instances, if the fifth string peg doesn't have a tendency to turn smoothly, this can be corrected by dismounting and cleaning it with metal cleaning fluid or silverware polish. If the inside parts of the peg are scarred, you can work these rough spots away with emery paper.

The geared pegs are not made for dismounting, but the tension screw should be kept adjusted in the same manner as the mounted fifth—string peg.

DRUM OR HEAD:

Your banjo head should be tight to get the best sound from your instrument. You will need a banjo wrench to tighten the bracket nuts.

In tightening the head, tighten the brackets a little at a time, proceeding clockwise, and keep repeating the process until the head is tightened to the proper degree. Watch the bridge closely, and when it is standing up fairly level, the head is about as tight as it will go without bursting.

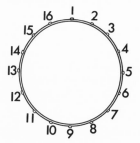

tightening the head

There should not be any loose brackets when the head is tightened. Another check to make is to look at the tension hoop. It should be level all the way around the shell.

A new calfskin head should have the tension increased over a period of several days for best results. They are affected by weather, and on damp days the bridge will sink into the head and the tone will be dull. You will then have to tighten the head, but if you forget to loosen the brackets on a dry day, the head may burst.

I personally prefer to use a plastic head, as it will hold practically the same level of consistency without changing with weather conditions. Since we perform all over the country in varying climates, I have found the plastic heads more suitable for my purpose.

The first time I used a plastic head, I was playing at a drive-in theatre, and the fog was so heavy that droplets of water were actually forming on the head. I was amazed that I could still pick away with the tone unchanged.

The tone difference between plastic and calfskin is negligible in my opinion, and therefore, plastic is preferable because of its other advantages.

BRIDGE:

A. A bridge comes in different heights and styles, three footed and two footed. The three footed bridge prevents sag in the middle.

B. The bridge should be placed so that any string fretted at the 12th fret will give a tone one octave higher than that same string played open.

You might wish to experiment with the bridge by sliding it backwards and forwards to see how it will affect the pitch and tuning. It might be suggested that you try swinging the 5th or 1st string end away from its parallel relation to the edge of the tail-piece for correcting one individual string that notes sharp or flat. Sometimes a set of strings will not note true, and the age of the strings will also cause difficulty in tuning.

C. The bridge should be set so the strings are about 1/8 - 3/16 inch above the fingerboard at the 12th fret. If the strings are too high, the instrument will be difficult to play, if they are too low, they will rattle and buzz.

This can be corrected by several methods, either adjusting the neck or the bridge. I would recommend that the neck be adjusted, as you will get used to one bridge height. If the neck is not adjustable, or has been adjusted as far as it can go, the bridge then could be altered. Raise the bridge by using strips of wood, and lower it by sanding off either the top or the bottom of the bridge.

ADJUSTING THE NECK:

Almost all banjo necks are adjustable. The location for adjusting is usually inside the "shell" or body, where the neck is attached.

If the neck is warped, and there is a tension rod in the neck, adjustment of this rod will correct the warpage. If your neck has such a rod, the adjusting nut will be found beneath a removeable plate, mounted on the peghead. I suggest that you let a professional repairman make this adjustment if you do not thoroughly understand how these adjustments should be made.

The neck should be fastened tightly to the shell, otherwise tone will be sacrificed, and the banjo will constantly be out of tune. Incidentally, the angle at which the neck meets the shell is 3°, but may vary slightly.

If the strings are too high off the fingerboard, an easy way to correct this, on some banjos, is to wedge a small strip of tin, or thin strip of wood, between the neck and tension hoop, thus slightly increasing the angle, thereby bringing the strings closer to the neck.

TENSION HOOP:

The tension hoop exerts pressure and tension on the head by the tightening of brackets. Be-

cause of the shape of present plastic heads, it is advisable to file down a portion of the hoop, as shown in the diagram, to avoid tearing of its mounting attachment.

SHOULDER STRAP:

A strap allows you to play while standing up, and you may find that holding a banjo while sitting is also aided by the use of one.

Adjust the strap while you are sitting, so that when you stand up, the banjo will still be in the same position relative to your arm, and your comfort in picking will be the same, whether sitting or standing.

STRINGS:

Strings should be changed when they lose their tensile strength and their response becomes dull. This may vary from one day to several months, depending on how much you play. String life can be lengthened considerably by wiping them off after playing.

My favorite type of strings are the Vega Scruggs-style strings, because of the life, tone, and brilliance — particularly of the wrapped fourth string, which outlasts the others that I have tried.

ARMREST:

An armrest adds to the comfort, keeps your arm off the head (preventing dampening of the tone), prevents the head from getting sweaty (which may rot a calfskin) and dirty.

RESONATOR:

All banjos do not have a resonator, but they are desirable when you are picking with a group of musicians, as the resonator amplifies the sound and directs it forward. I prefer the bowl shape to the flat type, because of the comfort and appearance.

TONE RINGS:

There has been a lot of controversy between the various types of tone rings, with varying opinions. One opinion that doesn't seem to vary, however, is that the flat-top type of tone ring gives a deeper tone than an arch-top ring. I feel that this is because of simple mathematics: There is less surface area of the head free to sound inside the ring of an arch-top ring, as shown in the diagram below.

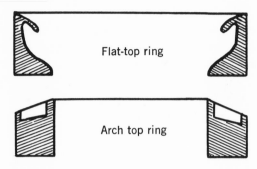

Flat-top ring

Arch top ring

It has also been found that the brass material seems to vary for an unknown reason, and therefore, two banjos with identical tone rings may vary greatly in their tone. It has been said that the metal tends to crystallize because of vibrations set up in the tone ring during the playing of the banjo. It seems, then, that the more the banjo is played, the more crystallization occurs, and a peak tone eventually comes to the banjo over a period of years. To me, a banjo either has the tone, or it doesn't. So why get so technical? My banjo has no alterations in any form.

It is also important that the tone ring fits well against the shell, and that it is not loose, or tone again will be sacrificed.

NUT:

If the strings are too high so that chording at the first position is difficult, the grooves in the nut can be deepened by carefully running a three cornered file through them until the depth is satisfactory. The strings should rest at the same level and in a tight fitting groove.

TAIL PIECE:

There has also been quite a bit of controversy in regard to the tail piece and tone quality, and especially concerning the weight of the material of the tail piece. I use a regular tail piece such as the ones made by Gibson and Vega.

One essential fact stands out in my experience. If it is too high, and you pick the strings very hard, the bridge will have a tendency to slip off center. If the forward part of the tail piece is too close to the banjo head, it will create very heavy tension on the head. This will mute and lower the volume of the banjo and will also bring the strings down too close to the fingerboard. The result will be a chattering or rattling of the strings when you are playing a chord. My theory on this situation is to have only enough tension on the tail piece to firmly hold the bridge in position.

CAPO:

My first capo consisted of a pencil with a rubber band attached at either end. Today there are fancier ones available. A capo is a great asset to the banjo. For instance, let's assume that a song plays well in a G chord, and although you want to sing the song in G, you find that it is too low for your voice. Let's assume that A would be a better chord for your voice. You can place the capo on the second fret from the peghead and play the song as though you were in G. This will then become an A chord. In other words, you can play in a new key, while holding the same finger positions of the chord used in G Tuning.

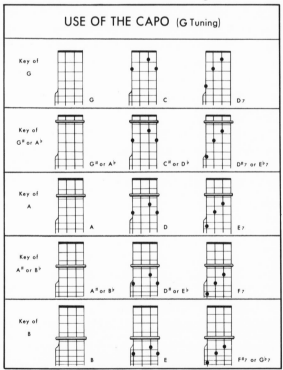

Use of the capo saves wear on the banjo neck. "A" tuning could also have been accomplished by tuning all the strings up two frets, rather than using the capo. However, this puts a strain on the neck, and tends to bow it. In our earlier recordings, we tuned up one fret to G#, to accompany our vocalist. As the years roll on, we find that the key of G works out better, to suit the deepening voice of the vocalists. When we used to tune up frequently, we observed bowing in our instrument necks, so we began to use capos, thus saving wear and tear on our instruments.

As you move the capo either higher or lower, the fifth string must be raised or lowered that same number of frets. To raise the string, you will have to tune it up, which puts a great tension on the small gauge fifth string. This may cause it to break occasionally, or to be stretched past its tensile strength, diminishing its response. This can be prevented by use of a small screw placed just behind the seventh fret, as shown in the diagram.

All you really have to do is slip the string under the screw, and the fifth string is automatically fretted at the seventh fret. When going from G to A tuning, simply slip the fifth string under the screw. When capoing up even further, for example, the third fret (Key of B flat), slip the fifth string under the screw, then just tune it up one more fret by hand. My banjo has a small hook, inserted like a spike or nail, instead of a screw. I, personally, made my own from one of my wife's hair pins. Similar ones can be purchased at hobby shops (miniature railroad spikes). There are, however, several slick adjustable 5th string capos on the market.

THUMB PICK:

You might wish to experiment with your thumb pick as I have done. I found that a thumb pick of lighter gauge plastic, with a point similar to the one in diagram A, gave a thinner and unbalanced tone. The one shown in diagram B is made of heavier plastic. I trim the point off as shown, and this gives me a fuller and more balanced tone.

However, you will want to experiment for yourself. A great deal of your tone will come from the angle of attack in which the pick hits or strokes the strings. This also affects the volume you will get from your banjo.

The amount of pressure you apply on the head with your ring finger and little finger will also affect the tone. But don't be overly concerned

with this in your starting stage as your main interest is to learn to pick. It will probably be best for you to experiment with this after you have learned to pick smoothly.

I have formed the habit of picking very loud and hard due to working in a group consisting of five or six people.

I have had some embarrassing moments when I would be playing away and my thumb pick would go flying out into the audience. And, unless I happened to have an extra pick, I was working under the handicap of an unbalanced hand and an unbalanced tone. I have corrected this to a certain degree by taking the sharp point of a pocket knife and cutting parallel grooves in the thumb pick. I cut them by holding the pick in the position shown.

This leaves the raised edge so the pick slips onto the thumb very easily, but it will not have a tendency to slip off your thumb.

I also clean and reshape the grooves as they become filled by accumulations from the thumb caused by perspiration and from continuous usage of the pick.

Reshaping of the thumb pick: Most thumb picks are made just a little out of twist, and often they are too large or too small to suit me. I correct this by using steam heat, or hot water. Heat the pick, holding it in hot water with Pliers, and then twist it into the position you desire, hold for a few seconds and the pick will remain in this position.

I prefer the National type picks for two reasons. They are made of lighter gauge material and have holes in them, as shown in the finger pick diagram.

The holes help a bit in preventing them from coming off. You may wish to reshape them as they are all made the same size. If the point is too straight for you, bend it to your specification. As you are picking, you may notice a roughness or scratching on the string. Since I perform while standing, and with a shoulder strap, I give the face of my picks a few brushes across the leather strap to free them of corrosion.

CHAPTER 3
Scruggs Tuners

I have had the question asked many times. What gave you the idea for the Scruggs Tuners? It came from a combination of past experiences with picking the banjo. My brother, Horace, and I used to sit around home working with ideas. One idea was to attempt to re-tune the banjo while playing a melody. I would re-tune my banjo, perhaps from a G into an open D. At any rate, I would often have a string or two a little sharp or flat and it was my duty to tune it as I played the song.

Later, from these sounds, I had the idea for quite awhile of making and mounting a tuner, but I had debated in my mind if it would really be worth drilling through the pearl inlayed peg-head of my banjo. Even though the sound was very different and attractive to me, I wasn't sure how my fans would take to the idea.

Another thing I did, which I don't recommend, was to give the neck an extreme push up, or pull down, while playing certain tunes. This is a threat towards breaking a banjo neck. Also, I gained knowledge from playing the banjo my father had which dis-corded very much. Some notes would note flat, so I would pull down on the neck. Others were sharp, and naturally I would push up on the neck. This reminds me of the old theory that you can make something good out of most anything if you try. I did learn something that I might not have thought of if I had been playing a better instrument.

I wrote and recorded "Earl's Breakdown" before I designed the tuners, de-tuning and re-tuning by ear, using the standard tuning pegs. I began receiving requests for this number on almost all of our performances and the decision was made to mount the tuners. It was a cam-type tuner which worked fairly accurately; it assisted the tune, to say the least. These first tuners were rather unsightly, so I covered them with a tin box, made from an old floor waxer. They are shown below in one of our old photographs. This reminds me — the little bit of metal cost me a new floor waxer.

"Earl's Breakdown" was first recorded October 24, 1951. I completed the tuners soon after the recording. "Flint Hill Special" was recorded, using the tuners, on November 9, 1952.

Almost all the major banjo companies, as well as many individuals, are or have made tuners from this idea. Some of them are sold as Scruggs-Tuners, and some are called by different names, such as winders, twisters, chokers, D-tuners, the whiners, risers, etc.

I would suggest that if you are interested in getting a set of tuners, you should consider all the different types that are available. If you feel you would like to make your own, go ahead. It's a very simple idea, but do give careful thought and care to the idea before drilling through your peg-head and possibly destroying the finish, and on many types of banjos, the pearl inlay.

(See Chapter 13.)

My good friends, Bill Keith and Dan Bump, have designed an advanced set of tuners called "Scruggs-Keith tuners" which are much more versatile and provide more accuracy than the cam-type tuners. Because the tuning mechanism and the tuning unit for each string are combined in a single housing, they are easily installed with pliers or a wrench in the standard peg-holes, and only four pegs appear on the peghead, leaving the traditional, uncluttered appearance. You don't have to drill extra holes in the peghead, running the risk of not drilling them straight, or destroying the pearl inlay of the banjo. These pegs tune the strings, and can be easily set to change the notes either up or down over any interval. They can easily be transferred from one instrument to another without leaving holes in the peghead where they were once installed. They can also be used for additional special affects, and for changing basic tunings, on the first and fourth strings. In my opinion, this type tuner is far superior to any cam-type tuner available, and this is the type that I now use.

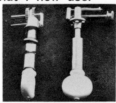
Cam-type tuners

Scruggs-Keith tuners dis-assembled.

Scruggs-Keith tuners mounted

CHAPTER 4
The Anatomy of Scruggs-Style Picking:

This Style involves the use of thumb, index, and middle finger of the right hand, which pick out various intricate and syncopated patterns of single strings.

The measures usually consist of eight 1/16 notes:

(FORWARD ROLL PATTERN)

But may consist of six 1/16 notes and one 1/8 note:

(BACKWARD ROLL PATTERN)

There are many "patterns" of eight 1/16 notes that constitute a measure. A few are shown below:

(ALTERNATING THUMB PATTERN)

(REVERSE ROLL PATTERN)

Other common timings found in measures in this style are:

Two 1/8 notes and four 1/16 notes:

Four 1/8 notes:

Also written as:

1 + 2 + 3 + 4 +

Of course, there are other ways of dividing up the measures. Some of the most common ones used have been illustrated.

Counting out loud could be helpful in learning the rhythm smoothly and evenly, but this could be a bad habit if it is continued past the early learning stage. For this style, count out loud: one-and-two-and-three-and-four-and, which will be written as 1 + 2 + 3 + 4 +.

A metronome is a handy thing to use instead of counting out loud since it provides a steady, constant rhythm. If you know someone who plays a piano, they most likely have a metronome and you can probably borrow one to use for awhile.

The exercises below are just for demonstration. Don't actually practice them now. They will appear in the exercise section later on in the book.

Practice with open strings first (G chord), so that you can concentrate on your right hand. Try this, but first I must remind you to anchor your ring and little finger for stability and accuracy:

1. (1) pluck down on the 2nd string with your thumb.

2. (+) pluck up on the 1st string with your middle finger.

3. (2) pluck down on the 5th string with your thumb.

4. (+) pluck up on the 2nd string with your index finger.

5. (3) pluck up on the 1st string with your middle finger.

6. (+) pluck down on the 5th string with your thumb.

7. (4) pluck up on the 2nd string with your index finger.

8. (+) pluck up on the 1st string with your middle finger.

In tablature, the measure you just played would be written as:

Now try counting it aloud, evenly and slowly, over and over:

1 + 2 + 3 + 4 +

NOW TRY THIS:

(1) Thumb plucks down on 3rd string.

(+) Rest.

(2) Thumb plucks down on 2nd string.

(+) Middle finger plucks up on 1st string.

(3) Thumb plucks down on 5th string.

(+) Index finger plucks up on 2nd string.

(4) Middle finger plucks up on 1st string.

(+) Thumb plucks down on 5th string.

In tablature, you would have just played this:

1 + 2 + 3 + 4 +

Now try the same thing while holding a C chord above with the left hand:

1 + 2 + 3 + 4 +

NEXT, TRY THIS (count out loud):

(1) Thumb plucks down on the 3rd string.

(+) Index finger picks up on the 2nd string.

(2) Thumb plucks down on the 5th string.

(+) Middle finger picks up on the 1st string.

(3) Thumb plucks down on the 3rd string.

(+) The strings are silent, but you say "and" aloud.

(4) Middle finger picks up on the first string, while at the same time, thumb plucks down on the 5th.

(+) Say "and" out loud again.

Repeat this measure over and over. In tablature, it would appear as:

This is the method by which the book will teach you to play. Of course, the counting (1 + 2 + 3 + 4 +) should only be used in the early stages. Don't get in the habit of counting all the time – it's difficult to count and sing at the same time!

The word "habit" can always be broken by patience and practice. Do not expect too much of yourself. At the same time, do not underestimate your ability. Take your time. Do these exercises over and over and over until after awhile, you will be doing them while thinking about something else.

CHAPTER 5

Tuning The Banjo:

In most three finger banjo picking, the key of G is used so that when all the strings of the banjo are played open, a G chord will be sounded. D tuning and C tuning are used occasionally.

TUNING YOUR BANJO IN G:

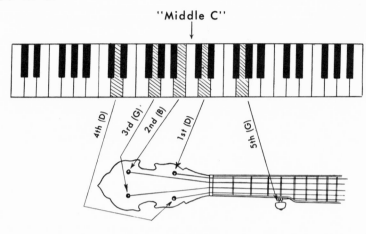

" G TUNING "

If a piano isn't available, a pitch pipe may be used. And if you have a fluorescent lamp, its hum is a 60 cycle B note—try that for fun. If neither of these are available, the following method can be used:

1. Tune the fourth string to a reasonable approximate pitch with your ear.   (D)

2. Fret the fourth string at the fifth fret and tune the third string to match the exact same pitch when they are played in unison (the third open, the fourth fretted at the fifth fret).   (G)

3. Fret the third string at the fourth fret and tune the second string to the same pitch.   (B)

4. Fret the second string at the third fret and tune the first string to this pitch.   (D)

5. Fret the first string at the fifth fret and tune the fifth string to the same pitch.   (G)   The fifth string gives a similar effect to the sound of a chord as a bagpipe, in that, it never changes its pitch unless noted. The fifth string is often referred to as the thumb string because it is practically always plucked with the thumb.

Uncle Dave Macon used to show the audience how he was taught to tune the banjo. It was in the form of a tune called "Children, Children, Come Home."

(D) (B)   (D) (B)   (G)   (D)
Chil-dren, Children, come home or,

(1st) (2nd) (1st) (2nd) (3rd)   (4th)
Chil- dren, Chil- dren, come home.

WHEN TUNING WITH A FRIEND WHO HAS A GUITAR:

1. Match your second, third, and fourth strings open to the same pitch as his second, third and fourth strings open.

2. Then use the previously mentioned method to tune your first and fifth strings.

C TUNING

C tuning is the same as G tuning with one exception. The fourth string is a C (one octave below middle C) and when the fourth string is fretted at the seventh fret, it will match the same pitch as the third string open.

D TUNING

1. The fourth string is tuned to the same D as in G tuning.

2. Fret the fourth string at the fourth fret and match the third string to that pitch. (F#)

3. Fret the third string at the third fret, and match the second string to it. (A)

4. Fret the second string at the fifth fret, and match the first string to it. (D)

5. I tune my fifth string to match the first string at the fourth fret, (F#) for a deep toned D chord.

Some people prefer to match it to the first string at the seventh fret. (A)

D MINOR TUNING:

The second and third strings are lowered two frets below their normal G-tuning pitch, (F and A) and the fifth string is raised two frets (A). An example of this will be found later in the book—"Nashville Blues."

MODAL TUNING:

1. Tune the banjo to G.

2. Raise the second string one fret. (C)

CHAPTER 6

Playing The Banjo — Basic Hints:

1. Before you begin playing, you will want to read the chapters about tablature, music reading, "The Anatomy Of Scruggs-Style Picking," and the Chord section.

2. Sit down and hold the banjo in the manner shown below, with the drum vertically placed. A shoulder strap will be necessary in order to play while standing, but you will probably find it easier to learn to play the banjo while sitting down.

3. With your left hand, try making the following chords. (G tuning will always be used in this book unless otherwise stated).

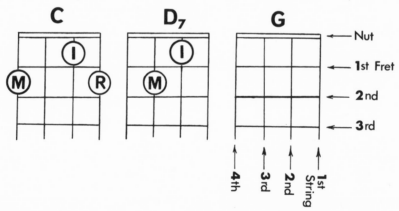

The circled letters tell which fingers of the left hand make the chords:

Ⓜ middle finger
index finger Ⓘ
Ⓣ thumb
ring finger Ⓡ
Ⓛ little finger

The letters above the diagram represent the chords.

4. The fingernails should be clipped short if they interfere with your playing, in order to come down cleanly upon the strings. Your fingers should come down perpendicular to the strings, firmly behind the frets. Your fingertips, at this time, should only touch one string apiece.

5. Brush down with your right hand across all the strings. If your left hand is holding the chord correctly, it should sound right.

Practice going from G to C to G to D7 to C to G, until you can change chords well, without hesitation. This will take a little practice to do clearly and smoothly.

Try strumming along with the following song, changing the chords as indicated. This is to develop practice in changing easily from one chord position to another.

MY CABIN IN CAROLINE

Words and Music by
LESTER FLATT and EARL SCRUGGS

(G)   (C) (G)

There's a cabin in the pines, in the hills of Caroline.

(G)   (D7)

And a blue-eyed girl is waiting there for me;

(G)   (C) (G)

I'll be going back some day, and from her I'll never stray,

(G) (D7) (G)

And the cabin in the hills of Caroline.

Chorus:

(C)   (G)

Oh, the cabin in the shadow of the pines,

(G)   (D7)

And the blue eyed girl way down in Caroline;

(G)   (C) (G)

Some day she'll be my wife, and we'll live a happy life,

(G) (D7) (G)

In the cabin in the hills of Caroline.

USE OF THE RIGHT HAND IN SCRUGGS-STYLE PICKING

Purchase a set of picks (two metal fingerpicks, and a plastic thumb pick) and place as in diagram (metal picks go on the index and middle finger).

(A) The Little Finger and Ring Finger:

The ring finger and little finger should be anchored against the drum so that the hand has stability and isn't flailing about. I find this essential for full stability. In experimenting, I found that my right hand is nearly twice as stable when both the fingers are anchored, rather than just one. Cut these fingernails short to keep them from cutting through the drum.

You should anchor those fingers in the position below, indicated by an "X .

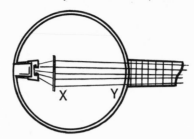

Note that if you play at Position "Y" (where the head meets the neck), you will get a deep, hollow tone, as compared to the sharp staccato sound when you play down by the bridge at position "X". This mellow tone heard by playing at "Y" is particularly effective when you are playing up the neck of the banjo and should be utilized then.

Even though all references hereafter will only emphasize the X and Y during your exercises with the right hand, check the tone changes between X and Y. You might find some attractive sounds between these two positions.

I might suggest that you pluck the strings along these positions hard, followed with a soft pluck. Repeat this without your ring finger and little finger touching the head. Through these methods of experimenting you will start, almost automatically, without concentrating on going to these positions for different sounds as you pick various songs.

This technique of playing at position "Y" is occasionally used in low neck positions for a measure or so, to get a particular effect, such as in "Ground Speed" or "Shuckin' The Corn".

"Ground Speed"

"Shuckin' The Corn"

(B) The Thumb:

The thumb always picks down, whereas the fingers pick up. I personally prefer to pick the melody notes as much as possible with my thumb. It is most capable of bringing out these stronger melody notes. I am a firm believer that the melody should be recognized above the other picking, as I mentioned earlier.

The thumb picks down on the fifth, fourth, third, second, and rarely on the first string (Example in "Pike County Breakdown"). When playing, the thumb should be extended as straight as possible.

(C) The middle finger picks up on the first string and rarely plays any other string.

(D) The index finger picks up on the second and third strings and occasionally on the fourth and first strings.

Your finger picks should pluck as flat as possible against the strings.

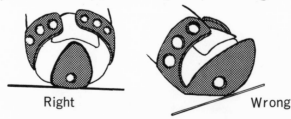

Right   Wrong

A REVIEW — FACTORS THAT AFFECT BANJO TONE

1. Banjo part adjustment:

    A. **Bridge:** A piece of pearl at the top of the bridge could have a tendency to give a sharper tone.

    A lighter bridge will also sharpen the tone.

    B. **Tailpiece:** Tension is important.

    C. **Head:** Tightness.

    D. **Strings**

    E. **Tone ring**

    F. **Resonator**

2. Playing Techniques:

    A. Position "X" and "Y".

    B. Dampening the head with fingers or palm mutes the tone.

    C. Plucking three strings strongly together gives an effect like using "hold" pedals on a piano.

    D. Use of fingerpicks: It will probably be to your advantage to begin learning to play with picks, although you may find this difficult at first. If you find the picks are holding you back, then side-track them. I learned without picks but it did take a short while to get used to them. My main interest is to help you to get started in the best way, and to the best of my knowledge.

    I am sure a lot of your ideas will be better than mine throughout this book. As a matter of fact, when I make a suggestion, I would like you to try it out; at the same time, take it merely as a suggestion and try your own ideas as you go along.

CHAPTER 7
Chords

To learn how simple chords really are, I suggest you study the chords in this chapter and you will soon see the point.

By making three chord positions, you will be able to play all the major chords by progressing up the neck of the banjo. Complications and confusion are most likely to arise when the 7th's, 6th's, #, and b etc., are used.

I designed the chart on the following page to start this simple idea. Follow the chart from the peg head all the way up the neck to the last fret. I believe after a few trips up the neck with a chord, even a 6th, 7th, etc., will come easy. In other words, in a matter of some thirty minutes, you'll be making all the chords in the book. This doesn't mean you will remember them all in this length of time. Even though they may come to you easily, do not underestimate the importance of them. Drill them into your mind until you can change chords without hesitating and with very little concentrating. I call this staying ahead of your music.

Chords will be used in vamping, and most of the time while accompanying singing and other musicians. Needless to say, quick changes will come along in many songs.

A chord is a combination of 3 or more tones or notes which blend harmoniously when sounded together. Note then, that an open 5th string can't be played with all chords (as previously mentioned), as there will be a clashing of tones, resulting in disharmony. The 5th string, in G tuning, will work in the chords of G, C, E flat, and E minor. See previous notes on use of the Capo.

Below are the three basic chord positions and fingerings which are used in the chart on the following page.

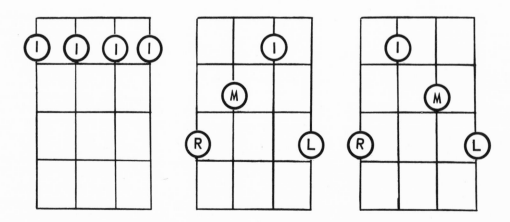

Note that while these same positions are held, the chord changes as you move up the neck (each fret changes the chord by one half step — in other words, as you advance one fret, you go up one half note on the scale).

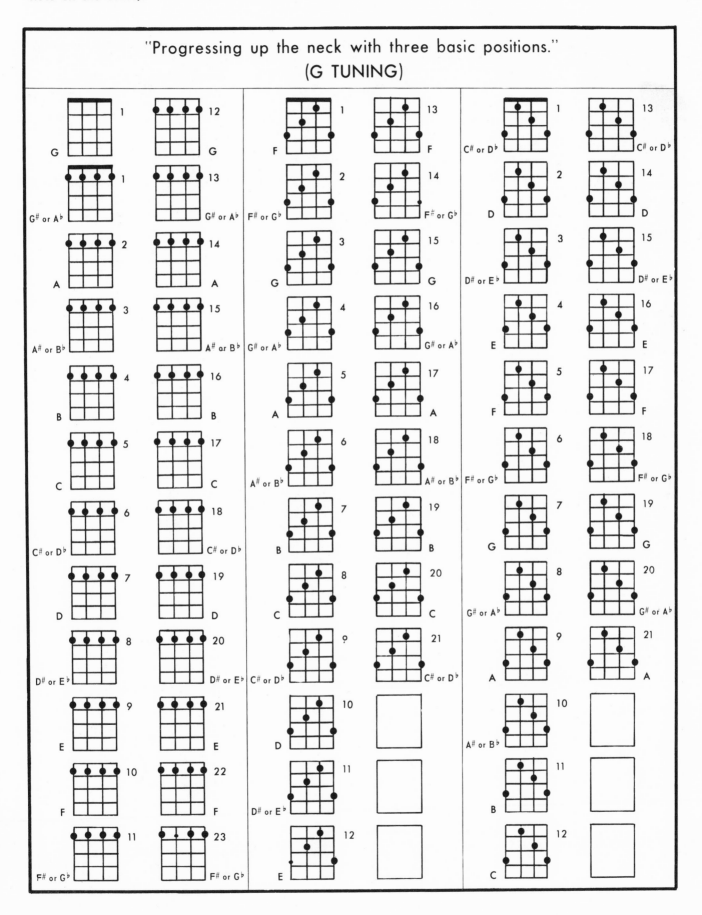

"Progressing up the neck with three basic positions."
(G TUNING)

As you looked at the basic position with the index finger on all four strings, you probably were trying to figure out how to split that finger into four equal parts. This isn't necessary. Just "barre" across with your index finger, as in the photographs below. When a 6th or 7th chord is called for, just reach up with the ring or little finger to get the note.

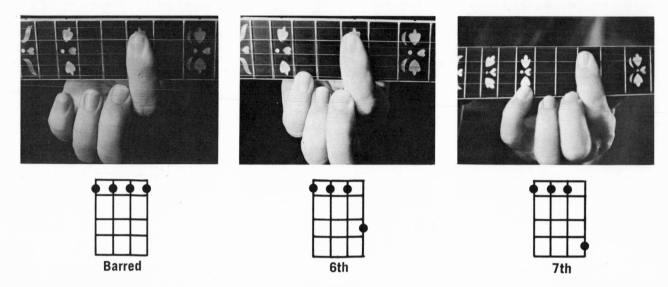

Barred   **6th**   **7th**

On the charts only major chords have been shown. It is my feeling that you will **understand** chords if you are shown how to form them, rather than learning a list of them by rote memory. It will be easiest to first show you a few basic principles on a piano (using the G chord), teaching you what sharp (#), flat (b), whole notes, and half notes are. Then, a complete study of the A chord on the banjo, compared to the piano, will teach you how to form any chord on the fingerboard at any octave position.

The **chromatic scale** is a progression, in order of tones, a half tone at a time:

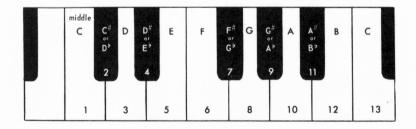

The Chromatic Scale

Starting at "middle C", count to the next C (one octave higher), noting that it is 12 **half steps** up, which is the same as 6 **whole tones.** Dropping one half note toward the bass notes—the deep pitched notes – is called **flat** (b). Raising one half note (toward the treble or high-pitched notes) is called **sharp** (#). Going back to the note (removing # or b) is called natural (♮). When a sharp (#) or a flat (b) sign is used in front of a note within a measure, that note is treated as such throughout the measure, but then becomes natural in the next measure unless indicated otherwise.

Examples of half steps (C to C#), (C# to D), (E to F).

Examples of whole steps (C to D), (C# to D#), (E to F#).

Now that you have this basic idea, here's how to make a chord:

1. **MAJOR CHORD**—consists of the "1st", "3rd", and the "5th".

   The "first" is the first note, and the actual name of the chord—i.e.—G
   The "third" is two whole steps up—B
   The "fifth" is 1½ steps up from the "third"—D

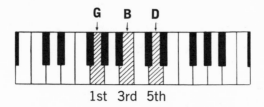

G MAJOR CHORD

2. **MINOR CHORD**—same as major chord, but the "3rd" is dropped ½ note (flat).

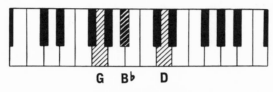

G MINOR CHORD

Minor chords are often abbreviated as (—) or (m) e.g. G— or Gm.

3. **AUGMENTED CHORD**—known also as the augmented 5th chord, because it's the same as the major, but the "5th" is raised ½ note (sharp). An augmented 5th is often abbreviated as a (+). For instance, G Augmented 5th may be written as: G+

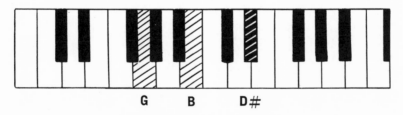

G AUGMENTED 5TH CHORD

4. **6TH CHORD**—same as the major chord, but a note is added. (The note a whole step above the "5th" is added):

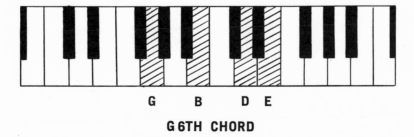

G 6TH CHORD

5. **7TH CHORD**—same as major chord, but a note 1½ steps above the "5th" is added:

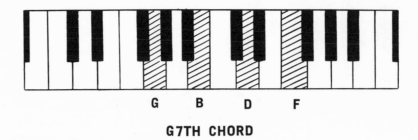

G 7TH CHORD

6. **DIMINISHED CHORDS**—any chord can be diminished by dropping all the notes (except the first) by ½ step (flatting them) Example—the G 7th chord above could be made into G Diminished 7th by lowering the "3rd", "5th", and "7th" by ½ step, and keeping the "1st" as it was.

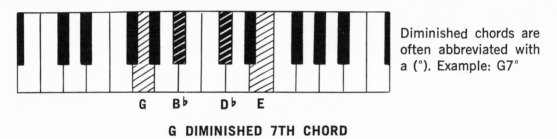

G DIMINISHED 7TH CHORD

Diminished chords are often abbreviated with a (°). Example: G7°

Now let's apply what you have learned to the banjo: In G tuning, an A major chord on the banjo is compared below to the same chord on the piano. Study the piano chord below to understand its components. Note that a lower "E" has been added, as it will be supplied on the 4th string of the banjo. An "E" is actually part of the chord, and therefore can be added by the 4th string to supply a full-sounding chord.

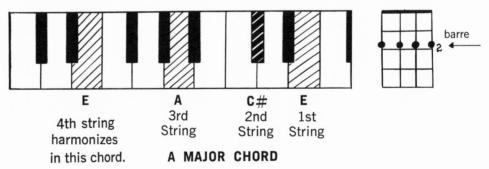

E
4th string harmonizes in this chord.

A
3rd String

C#
2nd String

E
1st String

barre

A MAJOR CHORD

To make this into A Minor, flat the "3rd".

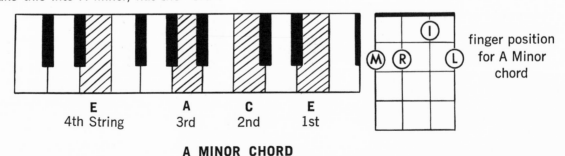

E
4th String

A
3rd

C
2nd

E
1st

finger position for A Minor chord

A MINOR CHORD

Now take the A Major chord and augment the 5th by making it sharp:

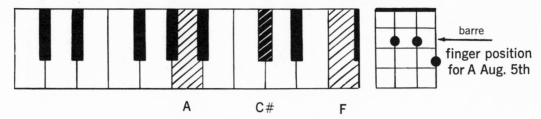

A   C#   F

A AUGMENTED 5TH CHORD

Note that the low "E" played on the 4th string in the major chord cannot be sounded in the augmented chord—as it would clash with the harmony of the chord. In order to use the 4th string, for a fuller chord, that low "E" must also be "augmented" to an "F".

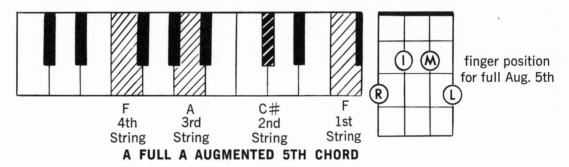

F   A   C#   F
4th   3rd   2nd   1st
String String String String

A FULL A AUGMENTED 5TH CHORD

Now take the major chord and add the "6th":

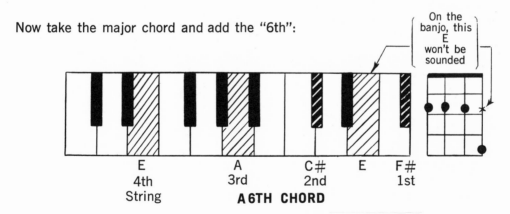

On the banjo, this E won't be sounded

E   A   C#   E   F#
4th   3rd   2nd   1st
String

A 6TH CHORD

Now try making an A7th Chord:

On the banjo, this E won't be sounded

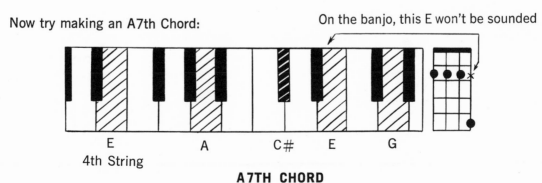

E   A   C#   E   G
4th String

A 7TH CHORD

Finally, try some diminished chords. Remember, all you have to do is flat all the notes except the first. Just barre with the index finger, one fret below the major chord, and get the other note(s) with other convenient fingers.

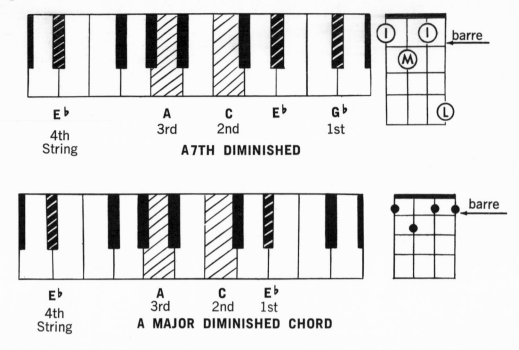

E♭
4th
String

A
3rd

C
2nd

E♭

G♭
1st

A7TH DIMINISHED

barre

E♭
4th
String

A
3rd

C
2nd

E♭
1st

A MAJOR DIMINISHED CHORD

barre

With the above information and chord charts, you should be able to form any chord on the banjo at any octave on the fingerboard, without memorizing, but understanding them instead.

Practical application of the above knowledge will teach you to form most chords, using proper fingering, so that you may travel swiftly and smoothly from any of the three major chord positions into their minors or 7ths, which are the principle offshoots from the major chords that are used in this book. Use the following, and practice going from major to minor, back to major, then to the 7th, then back to major again, until you can perform this series of movements smoothly, without tripping over your fingers:

MINOR   MAJOR   SEVENTH

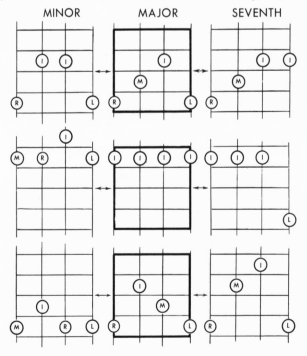

These positions apply to any fret level on the fingerboard

MAJOR CHORDS IN G TUNING

(G) D G B D *

The number beside each diagram indicates the fret.

* See text to work out minor 6th, 7th, augmented, and diminished chords

CHAPTER 8

How To Read Music

It is not essential to be able to read music in order to use this book as all the music is written in a much simpler tablature form which will be explained in the next chapter.

However, it is important that you learn timing, so it is my intention to teach you about timing in music.

First, the musical staff is divided into spaces by vertical lines, which are called measures. Each measure is equal in time value.

At the left end of each staff there are several symbols that should be explained. The spiral sign is called a "G-clef," and it circles the line on the staff on which the note G is placed. Just beyond this G-clef is the "Key signature," the group of sharps and flats that indicates the key in which the song is written. If the song is in the Key of C, there are no sharps or flats. (The principle key signatures you need to be concerned with in this book are: G—one sharp—, D—two sharps—, and C).

Just past the key signature is the "Time Signature." This is usually written as a fraction—e.g. 2/4, 3/4, 4/4. The lower number tells what kind of note gets one beat (quarter notes in the examples given here) and the upper number tells us how many beats to a measure.

A whole note (0) is the longest note, and is equal to four beats. For anything longer than that, you tie two notes together (00). A dot right after a note increases its time value by ½. A rest is a period of silence and has the same value as notes.

All the measures below have four beats in them. Use your arithmetic to verify this:

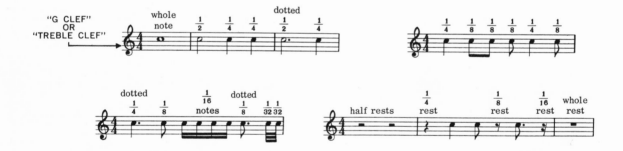

Study the above measures until you understand them, and why they are all equal in time.

My oldest brother, Junie, and my oldest sister, Eula May, were real fanatics about this business of keeping time. They used to begin playing a song together, such as "Sally Goodwin", then, while still playing, walk in opposite directions around the house until they met on the other side. If they were still playing the tune together, they would be satisfied their timing was up to snuff. (Try playing your banjo in time with a metronome, then walk out of the room while playing. Continue, walking back into the room to see if your timing is improving. Were you still in time with that metronome?) To this day, I don't know how on earth my brother and sister could tell who's timing was off if they came around the house not playing together—but with the metronome, we know who goofed!

Only C notes appear on the musical staff shown in the previous example. Each line and space between lines represents a degree of the scale on which musical notes are written, as shown below. Notes may be written above or below the staff by the use of small lines called "Ledger Lines," also shown below. Melodies being played one octave higher can be written on the same staff, and it is shown that they are meant to be played one octave higher by the sign: ⌐ 8 va. ⌐

Study the musical staff below, which demonstrates what was mentioned in the above paragraph. Then read the chapter on chords, which will help to clarify your knowledge of reading music.

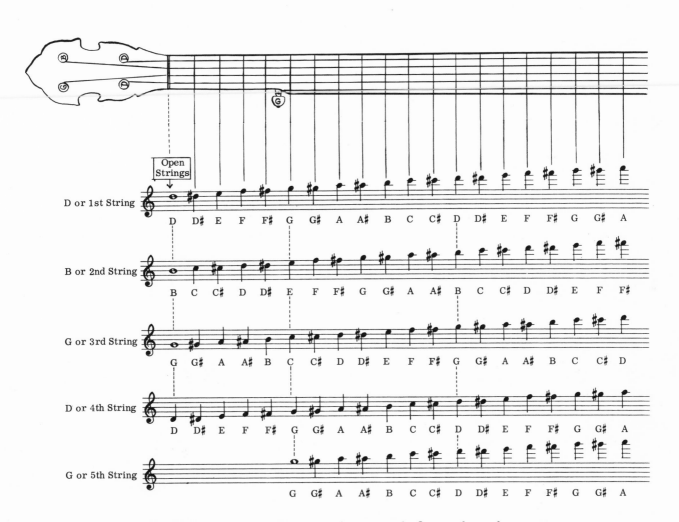

Chart of the fingerboard for the banjo

Following, are some other simple facts you will need to know about reading music:

A double bar is put at the end of a song, or a section within a song.

Two dots in front of it ⫶ means go back and repeat from the beginning, or

go back to the previous double bar where you will see two similar dots.

The sign: ⨟ means "repeat the previous measure." If there is a number over it, it means to repeat the previous measure a certain number of times.

Often when you repeat a musical phrase, the last measure will have this sign over it: (⌐1.) Right after the double bar will be a similar sign with the number 2. On repeating the phrase, when you come to the (⌐1.) skip it and go right ahead to the (⌐2.). In other words, the same phrase has two different endings.

CHAPTER 9

How To Read Tablature

What is tablature? It is a system of music writing that was used by lute players in the sixteenth century. A simplified version is used in this book. Without being able to read music (other than understanding timing) you can easily learn to play by reading the tablature which appears under the standard music notation.

Tablature is written on five lines which represent the banjo strings. The top line represents the first string of the banjo, the bottom line the fifth string. A number placed on a line (string) indicates the fret at which that string is to be fingered. An "O" means open string, not fretted.

Here is how it works. If your left hand were to make a C chord, tablature would describe it in this form:

And if you wanted to play a D scale for example, (do, re, mi, fa, sol, la, ti, do) starting on the fourth string and plucking each note with the thumb of the right hand, tablature would show it in this form.

do re mi fa sol la ti do

The method used to tell which fingers of the right hand are sounding the strings, or how they are doing it, is by indicating with letters above the tablature.

T = right thumb, plucking down.
I = right index finger plucking up.
M = middle finger plucking up.
B = brushing down across all or several strings. (The thumb is usually used for this.)
H = hammering on.
P = pulling off, or pushing off.
SL = slide.
CH = choke.

Use of tuners will be noted by ↓ or ↑ on the string depending upon tuning the peg up (↑) or down (↓).

Bar lines are used to divide tablature into "measures."

The Ⓒ means that the left hand is playing a C chord while the right hand is picking.

At times, more than one string will be sounded at once. Examples are given below to show how this will be indicated.

1. Brushing across all the strings with the thumb in a "C" chord would be indicated as:

2. Plucking the open first and fifth strings together with the middle finger (on first) and thumb (on fifth string) would be indicated as:

3. Plucking first, second and fifth strings together while the left hand holds a "C" chord would be represented as:

Hammering, choking, and other terms will be explained to you as you come to them in the book.

You are now ready to learn the "Anatomy of Scruggs Style Picking" and will utilize what you have learned in the previous chapters.

Actually, it would be almost impossible to teach you this style of banjo playing without the use of tablature, as music only tells you which note is to be played, whereas tablature tells you the manner in which the note is sounded, as well as the string it is sounded on, the finger that sounds it, and the pattern in which it is sounded.

To illustrate this point, one D note written in music form appears as:

Now look below, and see how many different ways this same D note can actually be arrived at while picking the banjo. Twenty-six possibilities are illustrated to drive home a point. The arrows point to the same D note.

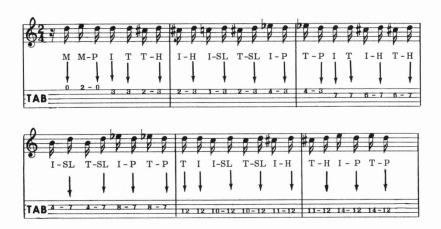

Below are a few measures in which you can pick out the same D note by use of the arrows again.

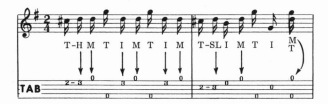

You can now see why it is necessary to use tablature to teach this style, along with the music. Music will be printed above the tablature so that you may try to correlate the two. Also, if you cannot read music, you may have a friend in your group who can read music and wants to accompany you on another instrument.

CHAPTER 10

Exercises In Picking

Before proceeding to the exercises in this book, it is important that you have already learned to read tablature, to count out a few basic measures, and are acquainted with your banjo.

The method I have devised to teach you to play is the easiest I can think of. You will start with the less complex basic patterns and techniques and eventually work up from there. Therefore, it is important that you tackle these exercises in the order that you find them in the book. It is important that you learn each exercise well before proceeding to the next one. Don't try to learn too much at one time. If it is only making a few chords, do that over and over until you can do them with very little effort.

The exercises in this section are designed to teach you the common basic patterns and techniques that I use. After learning them, you will find that any new patterns that you may come across will probably be variations of the ones you have already learned, or parts of other patterns pieced together.

In most cases, only portions of songs rather than whole songs have been used. The reason for this is to get you to concentrate on learning the patterns and how to use them within a song, rather than concentrating on merely learning the song itself.

Most of the fragments of songs used to teach will not serve as frustrations, since the whole song will appear in the song section of the book. A song may be played differently than heard on other recordings in order to demonstrate certain patterns and principles. However, the song as it appears in the song section of the book is, to the best of my knowledge, exactly the way I have played it on previous recordings. Following the song title, the album title will be given to enable you to refer to the song from which the tablature was taken.

Please go through the exercises slowly, being satisfied when you have learned them smoothly. Don't worry about speed. The beauty of picking lies in the smoothness and clarity of individual notes and not how rapidly you can rattle them off. Speed will come to you with time and practice so that you may use it when you find it necessary.

An album will be released with this book, or shortly thereafter, that will correspond with the exercises to follow in this section of the book. This will help you to hear and understand the lessons as you practice them. Although the complete tablature and timing is given, hearing the exercises will be most helpful for ease in learning them.

If you have difficulty locating the instruction album, feel free to write to me for information about it.

You are now ready to proceed to the first exercise.

EXERCISE I — BASIC RHYTHM

This exercise will teach you the basic foundation of a song. Even after you have become an accomplished banjo player, you will be using this basic rhythm as back-up when you are chording up the neck.

A "pinch" consists of picking down with the thumb (on the 5th string), at the same time picking up on the 1st and 2nd strings with the middle and index fingers. The use of the 2nd string here will get you in the habit of sounding the full chord. Later in the book, songs may show (by tablature) "pinching" with the thumb and middle finger only, but I would advise bringing in that index finger also, when the second string sounds good with the chord, and adds to the music.

With your banjo in G tuning, anchoring your fingers properly, try this, counting aloud, over and over:

(1) Thumb picks down on 3rd string
(+) Rest—the strings are silent, but you say "and" aloud
(2) "Pinch"—Thumb picks down on 5th string, middle finger up on 1st, and index picks up on 2nd string, all at the same time.
(+) Rest—say "and" aloud again
(3) Thumb picks down on 4th string
(+) Rest
(4) "Pinch" again
(+) Rest

Practice this over and over, counting it out. When it is smooth, add the C chord with the left hand, while still performing exactly the same with the right hand. When you add the D⁷ chord, "pinch" without the thumb, as the 5th string clashes with D chords in G tuning.

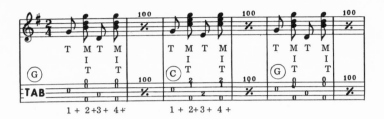

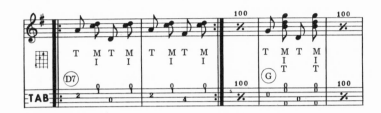

EXERCISE II — WORKING WITH THE THUMB

First, it will be necessary to limber up the fingers of your right hand.
    (1) Thumb picks down on 5th string
    (2) index finger picks up on 2nd string
    (3) middle finger picks up on 1st string

This is called a "forward roll." Do it over and over until you can perform it smoothly and evenly. Speed is not important at this time, only the smoothness of your technique matters.

I cannot overemphasize the importance of the thumb in banjo picking. Try the following alternating thumb pattern:

(1) Thumb picks down on 4th string
(+) Index finger picks up on 2nd string
(2) Thumb picks down on 5th string
(+) Middle finger picks up on 1st string
(3) Thumb picks down on 3rd string
(+) Index finger picks up on 2nd string
(4) Thumb picks down on 5th string
(+) Middle finger picks up on 1st string

Count this out loud, picking it slowly, but smoothly, over and over. It may seem difficult and cumbersome at first, but patience and practice will enable you to get this down smoothly. Notice that the D⁷ chord is omitted because of the disharmony of the 5th string.

This pattern begins your thumb working back and forth, readying it for its main role, to **carry the melody.**

Now let's try mixing exercises I and II together. Be sure to count out loud, and pick slowly:

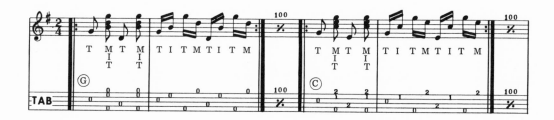

EXERCISE III — SLIDING

Sliding is a simple left hand technique that dresses up a tune with minimal effort. A slide is often used to open a tune, or to lead into a phrase within a tune. Sliding should be done with the middle finger of the left hand, as it is strong and maneuverable.

Fret the 3rd string at the 2nd fret. Pick the third string with the right thumb, then slide that middle finger right up to the 4th fret. The result is a slurred note. Repeat it again and again.

Now try sliding from the 2nd to the 5th fret on the 4th string.

Now apply sliding to the basic rhythm you have already learned:

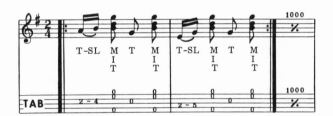

Next, try sliding with the alternating thumb pattern:

Next, mix sliding into exercises I and II combined:

When you are confident that you can do the above proficiently, you are ready for your first song,

CRIPPLE CREEK from "Foggy Mountain Banjo" album

Arranged by
EARL SCRUGGS

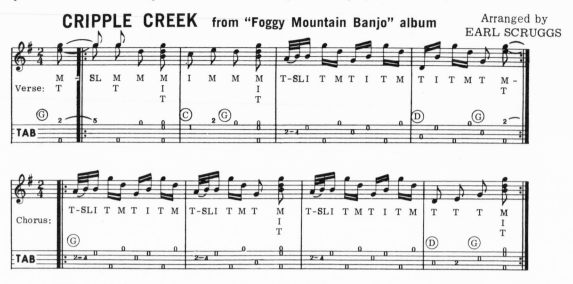

EXERCISE IV — HAMMERING ON

In playing the banjo, some notes can be sounded by the left hand. One method is to fret a string hard enough to make a sound. This is called "hammering on." For instance, pick the open 3rd string with the thumb of your right hand. Now bring the middle finger of your left hand down on that 3rd string just behind the second fret. When hammering on at first, you should bring that finger down upon the string from about ¾ of an inch above the fingerboard.

An open string isn't always involved. For instance, while fretting the second string at the 2nd fret with the index finger, you can hammer the middle finger down to the 3rd fret:

Don't attempt to learn this pattern at this time. It is merely illustrated to demonstrate a point. You will use it later. Try hammering into your basic rhythm:

Now try the following, slowly:

Using the middle finger of your left hand, add hammering into your alternating thumb patterns:

Now let's try adding this new technique to "Cripple Creek."

Arranged by EARL SCRUGGS

Before advancing to another left-hand technique, try a modification of the "forward roll." Practice these two patterns thoroughly:

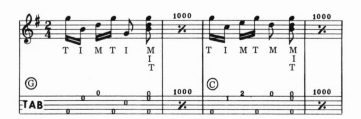

Now apply them to "Cripple Creek":

Arranged by EARL SCRUGGS

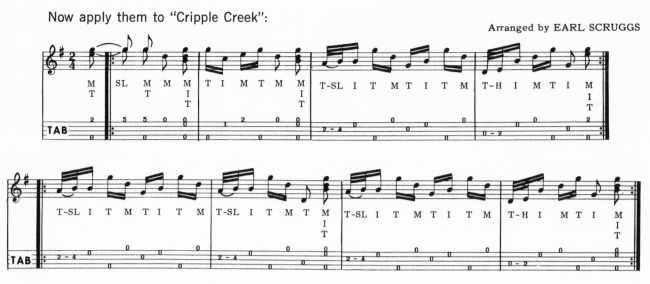

© Copyright 1966 by Peer International Corporation

By this time, it should no longer be necessary for you to count out loud, as you can play along with the record and grasp the rhythm from it.

EXERCISE V — PULLING OFF AND PUSHING OFF

Pulling off creates a very attractive sound. Its main purpose would come under the heading of assisting the right hand with the left hand. It brings out a different note from the string being plucked almost instantly, after the pluck of the right hand. This would practically be impossible unless the string is pulled off as shown in the illustration.

To do this, fret the first string at the second fret with your middle finger. Pick the first string with the middle finger of your right hand, then pull off the first string with your middle finger of the left hand. While doing this exercise, try to make the volume created by the left hand equal that of the right. Incidentally, I used to call this "picking with the left hand." This is a good left hand exercise, and will also be used in many tunes.

Pulloffs don't always result in an open string. Often you pull from one fret to another:

Don't practice this pattern now. It is merely for demonstration purposes, but you will use it at a later time. However, a good exercise to practice now involves **only** the left hand. Hammer down with your middle finger onto an open 1st string, then immediately pull off that same string:

Next, add pulling off to your basic rhythm:

So far we have just discussed pulling off. It is just plucking off toward the palm of the hand. Pushing off is pushing the string away from the palm of the hand, with the resulting sound being exactly the same as pulling off. When should one use which technique? It depends on the direction that the pulling or pushing finger (usually the middle finger) is traveling. For example, in the measure below, the middle finger of the left hand pushes off from the 2nd fret of the 3rd string, then travels to the 2nd fret of the 4th string. Then the right thumb picks the 4th string, which is now being fretted by that same left middle finger. Try this maneuver over and over:

Using the same pushing off technique, try the following pattern, over and over, aiming at smoothness and clarity of the notes:

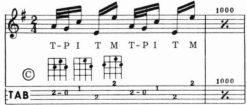

Now try the alternating thumb pattern. The first "P" represents a pulloff, the second "P" represents a pushoff:

Now try Cripple Creek again, using your newly-learned techniques:

Arranged by EARL SCRUGGS

Another useful pattern to learn is:

Try to use it now, in the chorus of "Cripple Creek":

Arranged by EARL SCRUGGS

Now try to play "Cripple Creek" as it is played on the **"Foggy Mountain Banjo"** album, but don't attempt the chorus variation or ending at this time.

CRIPPLE CREEK

Arranged by Earl Scruggs

EXERCISE VI — FORWARD ROLL AND REVERSE ROLL

There are many modifications of the forward roll that you will use, and you can probably think up a few more. Some of them are shown below, and will be useful to practice now:

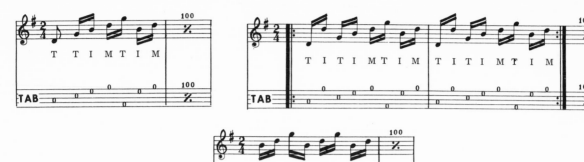

These patterns are all important ones that you will use commonly. The first one is an excellent pattern for working in the melody with the thumb.

The second pattern is also commonly used, and the last one is most typically used as a hammer pattern that will be in the "Advanced left hand technique section."

Another common forward roll is:

The "Reverse Roll" is sort of a combination of Forward and Backward Rolls. The Backward Roll (MITMITMITMIT) will be demonstrated at a later time. Try the Reverse Roll over and over, aiming at smoothness:

Using the last Forward Roll that you learned, and the Reverse Roll, try the first line of the "Ballad of Jed Clampett."

P. HENNING

There are many uses for the Reverse Roll. Note that in "Flint Hill Special," it is used many times. There are many ways that the preceding melody line could have been derived. Another example would be, use of the Basic Rhythm, Alternating Thumb, and Reverse Roll:

P. HENNING

"THE BALLAD OF JED CLAMPETT"

Come and listen to a story 'bout a man named Jed

This demonstrates the point that there are many ways to derive a melody or effect. By learning many patterns, and how to utilize them in a song, you will be equipped to play with a variety of techniques, so that your style will not become repetitious and hum-drum.

EXERCISE VII — BACKWARD ROLL

The backward roll is another useful pattern, and for some reason is difficult to do, unless practiced over and over and over. I often practice, almost without realizing it, on my knee. It is actually a good way to practice patterns, if you don't mind running the risk of being analyzed by observers!

This pattern is effectively used in "Home Sweet Home." Tune your 4th string down two frets, into C tuning, and try this first line:

Arranged by EARL SCRUGGS

Be it ev - er so hum - ble

Try this over and over, until it's smooth. You will note that "Ground Speed" also starts off with a backward roll. Now try the complete song of "Home Sweet Home."

HOME SWEET HOME

(C tuning)

Arranged by Earl Scruggs

One exercise you might find helpful in reviewing the rolls you have learned was shown to me by Bill Keith: Fret the first string at the fifth fret, and the second at the eighth fret (both these notes will be G). Now, using the right thumb on the fifth string, the index on the second string, and the middle finger on the first string, practice your whole vocabulary of rolls — the forward, backward, reverse, alternating thumb, and any other pattern that occurs to you.

It is best to practice this exercise when there is nobody else around — the fast series of G notes produced could prove to be very aggravating to anybody listening, even to yourself! The purpose of this exercise is to smooth out the rhythm of your playing — the duration between the notes should be the same, and the intensity or loudness of each note should be the same. Also, if you change continuously from one roll to another, you will gain a fluency in varying the type and order of the patterns which will improve your playing. And if you do this exercise with a metronome, you will reap added benefits.

A diagram of the left hand position and a sample series of rolls follow:

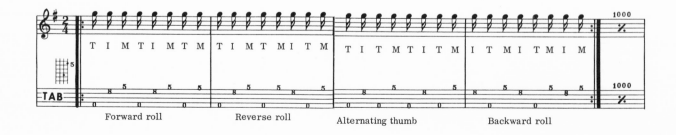

Forward roll   Reverse roll   Alternating thumb   Backward roll

EXERCISE VIII — ADVANCED LEFT-HAND TECHNIQUES

You now have the basis of the most important patterns I use if you have practiced them diligently. Next, you will see how it is simply a matter of adding left-hand technique to the already learned right-hand patterns, to add to your "vocabulary of banjo licks."

First, try this pattern. The pattern is sort of a "reverse roll pattern":

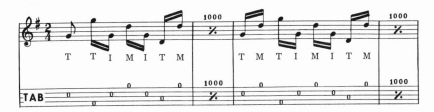

When you are satisfied that you have this pattern down well, try this next one, over and over. It is a very important "lick," and must become so familiar to you that you can do it without thinking about it:

Note that while the middle finger of the left hand is sliding from the 2nd to the 4th fret, the 1st string is simultaneously being sounded by the right middle finger:

This pattern will have to be practiced thoroughly, to become a part of you. Listen to it carefully to see how it should sound. It is often used to end a passage within a song, and it is even employed to begin a passage on occasions, such as in "When I Left East Virginia," which can be heard on the album **"Hard Travelin'—The Ballad Of Jed Clampett."**

Another lick which I commonly use to end a passage is shown at this time, but I would prefer that you hold off until a later date to try and learn it:

For review, practice sliding with the alternating thumb pattern, over and over:

Now try the forward roll, using hammering as shown below:

In performing these hammer-patterns, the second string should be fretted by the index finger of the left hand (at the 2nd fret), then hammer to the 3rd fret with the middle finger.

Next, try using a hammer and a pulloff (or a pushoff, as the case may be) in the Reverse Roll. It is another widely used pattern:

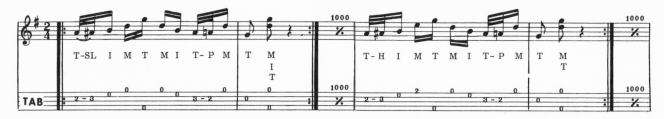

At this time, try playing "Flint Hill Special," which is made of these new "Advanced left-hand Technique" patterns. (pg. 102).

EXERCISE IX — "FILL-IN LICKS"

As you finish a melody break on the banjo, there is often a pause until the vocalist comes in, or until another instrument comes in for a break. During this time, the banjo adds a few subtle remarks. I shall try to give you some examples to work with.

A simple one can be heard at the end of the first banjo break in "Hot Corn, Cold Corn," from the **"Carnegie Hall"** album. This same lick can be heard in the opening break in "My Wandering Boy," "Blue Ridge Mountain Home," "My Cabin in Caroline" and "When I Left East Virginia."

On the **"Carnegie Hall"** album, listen to "Yonder Stands Little Maggie." The fill-in at the end of the breaks is a lick that can be repeated as many times as necessary (indicated by an "X"), until the vocalist comes in:

This same lick could be done up the neck, and would go like this:

The ending which is heard at the end of the first banjo break in "Salty Dog" from the **"Carnegie Hall"** album and is also used at the end of the banjo breaks in "Roll in My Sweet Baby's Arms" and goes like this:

At the end of the second banjo break in "Salty Dog," another lick is used:

This lick is also used at the end of the first break in "Your Love is Like a Flower."

A catchy little lick that can be repeated over and over is given below. An example of this can be heard on the **"Carnegie Hall"** album, at the end of the backing of the opening fiddle break in "Footprints in the Snow," and in "I Wonder Where You Are Tonight."

Another way to get a similar sound is:

Of course, there are many possibilities. Several more are shown below:

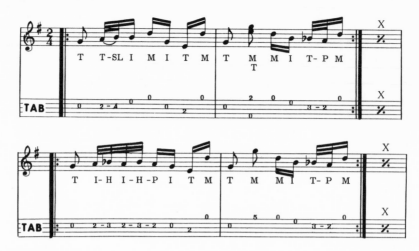

The latter is commonly used, and can be heard at the end of the opening break of "Hello Stranger," "Doing my Time," "Down the Road," and in the last solo break in "Your Love is Like a Flower."

LEADING INTO A BREAK

There are certain licks that can be used to lead into a passage. For instance, the following is used while waiting for the vocalist to come in on the **"Ballad of Jed Clampett"** album.

Another effective lead-in, commonly used, is:

A very effective lead-in can be done on the first two strings, such as in "Wreck of the Old '97," from the album **"Hard Travelin'."**

A hammer-on is a very effective lead-in, such as in "Earl's Breakdown," in the **"Foggy Mountain Jamboree"** album:

EXERCISE X — WALTZ RHYTHM (3/4 TIME)

Occasionally, you will want to do a number in ¾ time, such as in common old favorites like "On Top Of Old Smokey," "Sweet Betsy from Pike," etc. Try the following exercises before attempting any songs in this timing:

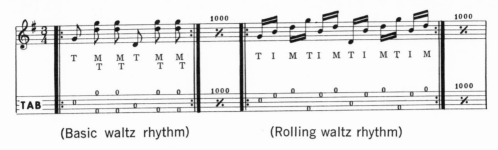

(Basic waltz rhythm)   (Rolling waltz rhythm)

Now combine these exercises, then add a slide:

Next, try hammering and pulling into these patterns.

Now that you have practiced these exercises, capo up two frets, and try "Good Times are Past and Gone," as the opening break is played in the album **"Folk Songs Of Our Land."**

GOOD TIMES ARE PAST AND GONE (A Tuning)   LESTER FLATT and EARL SCRUGGS

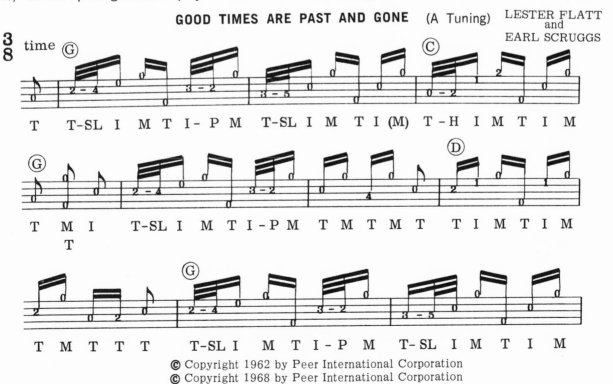

© Copyright 1962 by Peer International Corporation
© Copyright 1968 by Peer International Corporation

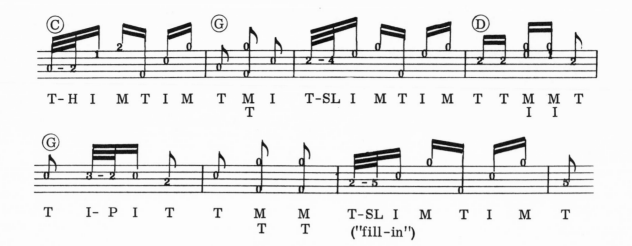

T–H I M T I M T M I   T–SL I M T I M T T M M T
    T   I I

T I–P I T T M M T–SL I M T I M T
           T   T ("fill-in")

GOOD TIMES ARE PAST AND GONE

LESTER FLATT and EARL SCRUGGS

1.

Ⓖ   Ⓒ Ⓖ

I wish to the Lord that I'd never been born,

      Ⓓ

Or died when I was young;

Ⓖ   Ⓒ Ⓖ

I never would have seen your sparkling blue eyes,

     Ⓓ Ⓖ

Or heard your lying tongue.

CHORUS

Ⓖ   Ⓒ Ⓖ

All the good times are past and gone,

      Ⓓ

All the good times are o'er;

Ⓖ   Ⓒ Ⓖ

All the good times have past and gone.

     Ⓓ Ⓖ

Little darling, don't you weep no more.

2.

Ⓖ   Ⓒ Ⓖ

Now, don't you see that lonesome dove,

      Ⓓ

Flying from pine to pine?

Ⓖ   Ⓒ Ⓖ

He's mourning for his own true love,

     Ⓓ Ⓖ

Just like I mourn for mine.

3.

Ⓖ   Ⓒ Ⓖ

Now, can't you see that lonesome train,

      Ⓓ

Going around the bend?

Ⓖ   Ⓒ Ⓖ

He's taking away my own true love,

     Ⓓ Ⓖ

To never return again.

EXERCISE XI — SCRUGGS TUNERS

At this point, I would suggest that you go back and review Chapter 3—"Scruggs Tuners."

I have used the tuners in several of my recordings. You can hear them in "Flint Hill Special," "Randy Lynn Rag," "Foggy Mountain Chimes," all in the album **"Foggy Mountain Jamboree."** Occasionally, single use of a peg is very effective, such as in "Bound To Ride," on the album **"Hard Travelin'."**

TUNING

The usual setting of the tuners is as follows: in the normal position, a G chord is produced (the third string sounds a G and the second a B) and in the lowered position, a D chord is produced (the third string sounds an F# and the second string is A). This setting is used for all the tunes mentioned above except for "Randy Lynn Rag." In this tune, the second string produces a B in the normal position, and raises the string to C when it is operated. The third string peg is set the same for "Randy Lynn Rag" as in the other tunes.

PRACTICING WITH YOUR TUNERS:

After getting them in tune, try out each peg. Pick the 2nd string with your index finger, right hand, then immediately turn the tuner down until it stops. Turn it slowly to make the slurred sound last the full length of its musical notation. Pick the 2nd string again, slowly turning the peg back up until it stops. Try this same maneuver with the 3rd string, picking it with your right thumb.

"Flint Hill Special" is opened in the following manner:

The tuner breaks throughout the song differ by one note:

The use of the tuners in "Earl's Breakdown" and "Bound to Ride," is done by stroking the string, then detuning, then retuning, in one continuous slur. Tablature describes this use in "Earl's Breakdown" in the song section in the book. Try practicing the following:

EXERCISE XII — HARMONIC CHIMES

Very pretty sounds can be made on the banjo, called harmonics, and commonly known as chimes. Listen to "Bugle Call Rag" on the **"Foggy Mountain Banjo"** album. The bugle call used in this song is an example of harmonics. Another example in the same album, is the ending of "Reuben." "Foggy Mountain Chimes" on the **"Foggy Mountain Jamboree"** album is still another example of harmonics within a song.

How is this done? Rest your finger (preferably the ring or little finger of your left hand) upon the 1st, 2nd, 3rd, and 4th strings at the 12th fret. Without depressing the strings, pluck the 1st string with your right middle finger. As soon as you pluck the string, immediately remove the left hand, or else the vibrating string will be dampened as it vibrates against your finger. The reason for the use of the ring or little finger of the left hand, is that this will leave you in good finger position to go into the song after playing the harmonic chimes. Try chiming on the other strings, using appropriate fingers, still at the 12th fret.

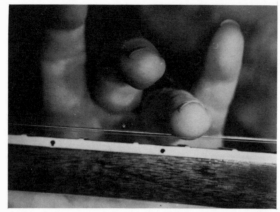

In most instances, you will be resting your barred finger across all four strings, as you will be playing a series of harmonic notes on these strings. Because of rapid tempo, it will be difficult to release your finger off the strings after each note, but a reasonable chime can still be heard.

Try playing a bugle call on the 12th, then on the 7th fret:

At times, single notes within a melody are effectively performed, using harmonics, such as in "Foggy Mountain Chimes."

Harmonics make effective endings for certain songs. A simple "pinch" of harmonic chimes is one example:

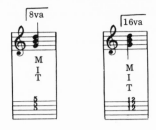

The harmonic ending of "Reuben" (D tuning) is done on the 5th fret:

That last chimed note is slurred by giving an extreme push down on the drumhead with the little and ring fingers of the right hand, or by a push up of the neck by the left hand. To get this effect, I would recommend the former, as the latter technique is a threat towards breaking the neck.

Harmonic chimes will only work at certain fret positions, the common ones being 5, 7, 12, and 19. A brief and interesting explanation will show you why chimes can be sounded at these frets, and how you can find other positions where chimes can be sounded:

If you read the chapter on chords, you should have some idea of what a chord consists of, and what harmony is. There is an actual mathematical reason for the harmony in the "1 - 3 - 5" of a major chord, and why the sound is pleasing to the ear.

The transmitted vibration of a banjo string is not a simple sound wave (∿∿∿), but is a sound wave accompanied by a series of smaller sound waves (minor vibrations) called overtones:

OVERTONES

Using the above described technique, play a harmonic at the 12th fret (the note you get will be an octave higher than the note sounded when the same string is played open). If you try it on the 11th or 13th fret, you won't get a chime. Why?—because the 12th fret is exactly ½ the scale. (Measure the distance between the nut and the bridge, and you'll find that the 12th fret is the halfway point.) Now divide the scale of your banjo into thirds. You'll find that 1/3 of the scale, starting at the nut, lies at the 7th fret, and 1/3 of the scale from the bridge end, lies at the 19th fret. Try them—you'll find that they are the identical chime sound—a note 1/5 higher than heard at the 12 fret chime. Next, divide your scale into fourths. You'll find that the fourth at one end is at the 5th fret, and at the other end lies up past your fingerboard, as shown in the diagram on the following page by a dotted line. This note is two octaves higher than the open string.

To carry this even a step further, divide the scale into fifths. One chime is just below the 4th fret, the other is way past the fingerboard, up on the head, as shown in the diagram by another dotted line. This note is even a third higher. You can now see why the "1 - 3 - 5" of a major chord harmonizes—the "3" and "5" of the chord reinforce the overtones of the basic note, "1".

I have found a few other locations where the strings will chime. At this point, I really don't have a logical reason to offer, but I really have a tendency to believe that everything to date has not been figured out about this instrument. For instance, a chime at the 9th fret is a B chord, the same as a chime at the 4th fret.

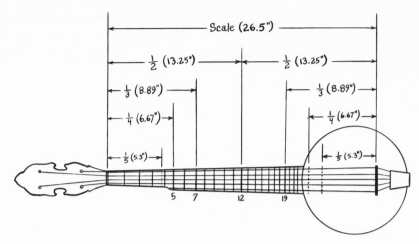

This harmonic demonstration shows the principle tones you hear when plucking a string. Now that you might understand harmonic chimes more clearly, go back and practice them. I hope you'll enjoy playing them even more so than before.

EXERCISE XIII — RHYTHM AND "BACK-UP"

Up to now, you have learned to take a melody break on the banjo, and you have learned a few "fill-in licks" that bridge the gap between the end of your break and the beginning of the vocalist or other instrumental break. But what should you be doing during their break? This falls under the category of rhythm and "back-up." In other words, you are going to "back-up" the other musicians and try to complement their music.

I have been asked over and over again why I back-up certain songs high on the banjo neck or in a low position. My answer to this question will take some explaining. I usually play or pick what I feel, but there's a reason for it. By this, I mean that if a song is being sung in a low tone, I feel that a high-pitched chord on back-up is an asset, or vice versa, because of simple harmony. For instance, when a song is being sung, if the melody is played in unison with the singer, it becomes a bit boring. To define this subject a little closer, it compares with two people conversing. If they had the same story to tell, they would not try to tell the story together. One would tell the story, and the other, who perhaps might know the story word for word, would only fill in a few details, not to take from, but to make the story a little more attractive and interesting.

When the fiddle, dobro, or guitar player is taking the lead part, I often play a rhythm pattern, then they play the rhythm when I take a lead break. Occasionally a picking back-up is effective during the vocal break, and is utilized. An example of this may be heard on the **"Hard Travelin'"** album, in "Wreck of the Old '97."

In backing-up, my full intentions are to fill in details while the featured artist is pausing for his or her next line. This is up to you to decide when the artist or the song will need this added touch.

When playing rhythm, several essential points are worth noting. This will be the first time that you will be really utilizing high neck positions . When playing rhythm up the neck, it is essential that you **form full chords,** as open strings played while you are in a high neck position would be in the wrong octave, and would sound out of place, though you may occasionally have to try to get away with it during fast tempos and rapid chord changes.

Another point to bear in mind is the use of "X" and "Y" positions, which were explained earlier in the basic instructions in the book. Compare the use of these positions to the use of the pedals on the piano. Without use of the pedals on the piano, a piece would become dull and lose its accentuation. The "X" and "Y" are the "pedals" of your banjo! Use them, particularly during rhythm and back-up.

Another technique is called "muting, dampering, or dampening". There are several ways of doing this. One is to press the chord with the left hand about half-way down to the frets, not letting the strings quite touch the frets. Pluck three of the strings at the same time with the right hand, or more than three strings by letting the fingers pluck off the three strings onto the other two strings, thus sounding all strings. Another method is to let the left hand press the strings against the frets, then release the strings so that the strings will be about half pressed down. This will make the chord sound, and will also give a muffed effect. I sometimes call these above described methods "vamping" rhythm.

Try both of the described "vamping" rhythms in G, C, and D chords, using the basic chord position. Be sure to **hold the full chord!**

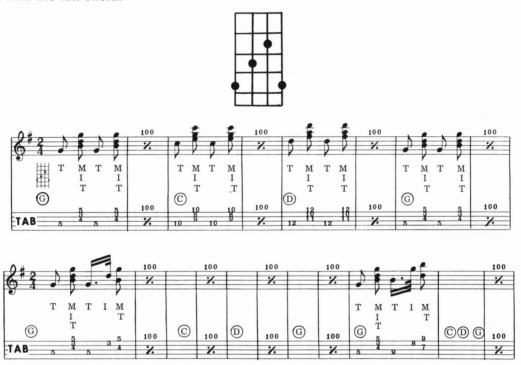

Now repeat this exercise, but press the bass (4th) string all the way down, so that it sounds each time the thumb picks it. Release it halfway after sounding it to benefit in a full "vamp" effect when you pluck the other three strings together, then push it down again each time you strike the string in order to sound it. The effect will be a vamping rhythm, containing a sounded bass note within.

Next, try this vamping rhythm pattern, without pressing the bass string for full sound. Two methods of obtaining the same rhythm in the G chord are given. Try both of them, then apply this same rhythm to the C and D chords, holding the same basic chord position with the left hand.

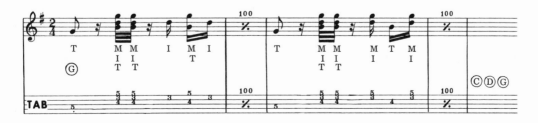

Examples of this type of vamping can be heard as the dobro is coming in for a break on "When I Left East Virginia," on the album **"Hard Travelin',"** and also in "Take This Hammer" on the **"Carnegie Hall"** album.

Repeat the same vamping pattern, but this time, sound the bass string. Examples of this common rhythm pattern are heard during the fiddle breaks in "Flint Hill Special" and "Footprints In The Snow" on the **"Carnegie Hall"** album.

Next, add a hammer to these vamping patterns. Your left index finger will get a workout, and is the only moving left–hand finger during this exercise. The left-hand changes are shown above the G chord exercise. Apply this to the C and D chord also:

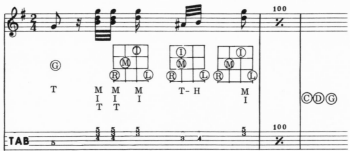

During all of these vamping exercises, you will note that the 5th string hasn't been sounded. By accident, you may strike it during sounding of the 4th string. If you aren't holding a chord that this high G string harmonizes with, you will be very embarrassed and will probably turn a beautiful shade of red if you accidentally strike the 5th string at such an occasion during a performance. There are two ways out of this. One is to say, " 'scuse me," but the other is more recommendable. The other way is to rest the base of your right thumb against the 5th string while "vamping," so that if you accidentally sound it, the tone will be muted and unnoticeable. Try this out, hitting the 5th string on purpose, and try to get in the habit of utilizing this technique.

To better benefit yourself with rhythm, try playing with other musicians. A guitar player will be a good asset, and an old-time fiddler would be most helpful. A very useful method of learning to apply these back-up exercises would be to get in tune with a record, and play back-up right along with the song.

A very simple, but effective back-up consists of "vamping" with use of a few bass string notes that lead into each chord change:

If you listen to the back-up during the fiddling of "Cripple Creek" and "Cumberland Gap" (on **"Foggy Mountain Banjo"** album), you will hear a mixture of vamping, sliding, and a few melody notes and lines. The sliding is accentuated by use of the "Y" position. The first few lines of back-up heard during the second fiddle break in "Cripple Creek" are duplicated below in tablature, as accurately as possible, by listening to the recording.

Arranged by EARL SCRUGGS

"Vamping" may even serve as an ending, such as in "Flint Hill Special."

It was previously mentioned that occasionally you can pick while someone is singing or another musician is playing a melody, without offending them. A good harmony principle to remember is to play low notes when the vocalist's melody goes high, and make your runs move up the scale when the vocalist does the opposite. The best example of this is in "When I Left East Virginia" in the **"Hard Travelin'"** album. The opening singing lines are given as they correspond with the banjo back-up. Listen to the record to fully understand the explanation.

LESTER FLATT and EARL SCRUGGS

Below is the banjo back-up that is played during the first vocal break of "Wreck Of The Old '97," on the **"Hard Travelin'"** album. Although the passage below contains no melody notes from the song, it is still effective as back-up for the tune. Similar picking can be heard during certain breaks in "Dixie Home," **"Hard Travelin'"** album; fiddling breaks of "Lonesome Road Blues" (**"Foggy Mountain Banjo"** album); "Take Me In A Lifeboat," and "My Little Girl In Tennessee," both in the album, **The Original Sound.**" A good slow number to hear this type of back-up is "No Mother Or Dad," in **"The Original Sound"** album.

Picking can be effective high up the neck also. The "Y" position should be utilized, and a simple roll (TIMTIMTIM) is used. The 6th chords are used by fretting the 5th string with the thumb. The 7th chord is also used frequently. (Just move the thumb up one fret.)

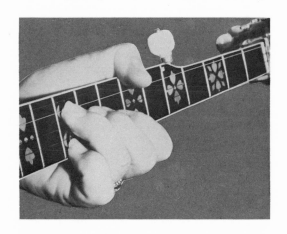

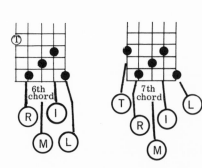

The example below is the forward roll done with a C6th chord. Try the G6th and D6th chords also. An example of this type of back-up can be heard in "Blue Ridge Cabin Home," on the **"Foggy Mountain Jamboree"** album; "No Mother Or Dad," "Martha White Theme" and "Hot Corn, Cold Corn," the last two in the **"Carnegie Hall"** album, and in "Dixie Home," on the **"Hard Travelin'"** album.

The backward and reverse rolls for example can also be used with both the 6th and 7th positions. A little experimenting here will point out many variations of this lick.

While you are listening to this type of back-up, you will hear a catchy lick used quite often. Listen to "Blue Ridge Cabin Home." This is how the lick is done:

A catchy lick that can be heard as back-up in "My Cabin in Caroline" and other tunes is as follows:

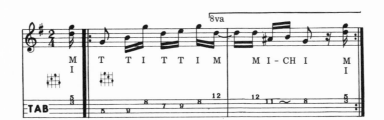

"Boogie-Woogie" back-up can be fun to do, and I occasionally use it. Example songs are "Footprints in the Snow" **"Carnegie Hall"** album, and "Down the Road," **"Country Music"** album. Try this:

When only the first two strings are being played, it is desirable to mute the 3rd, 4th, and 5th strings by resting the thumb on the 4th and 5th strings, and resting the tip of the thumb against the 3rd string. This will mute these strings, thus preventing non-harmonizing resonance from occuring. The "Y" position must also be used to obtain the mellow effect. These principles apply to the next type of back-up, which is also done on the first strings, using only the middle and index fingers. This type of back-up is very effective in slow tunes, some of which are: "This Land is Your Land" **(Folk Songs of Our Land)**; "I'll Just Pretend" on the **"Country Music"** album. Below is an example, heard in "This Land is Your Land":

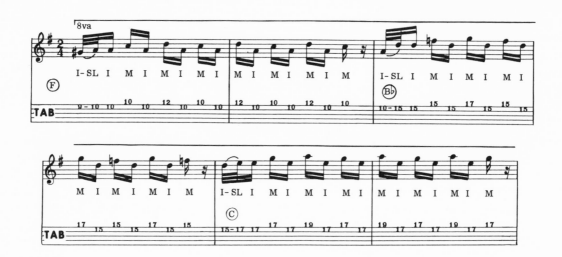

This same type of back-up applies well to ¾ time, but remember, there are only six ⅛ notes instead of eight ⅛ notes. Examples of this type of back-up in ¾ time are "Good Times Are Past And Gone" in the album, **"Folk Songs Of Our Land"**, "Bummin' An Old Freight Train," from the album, **"The Fabulous Sound of Flatt and Scruggs"**; "Over The Hill To The Poorhouse" from the album **"Hard Travelin'."**

Occasionally, a run of harmonics can be effectively used for back-up. The best example is in "Cora Is Gone" (D tuning) in the album, **"The Original Sound."** The harmonics in this song are done on the 5th and 7th frets. Another example of this is in "Doin' My Time" from the albums: **"The Original Sound,"** and **"Country Music."**

A recent type of back-up has crept into my repertoire, and, as you can hear and recognize, was inspired by Floyd Cramer's piano back-up heard on many records these days. Listen for this lick in recent recordings:

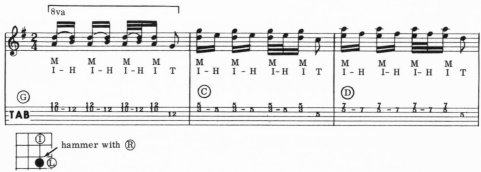

The finger position is the same wherever you use the lick: Listen to some of Floyd Cramer's piano work to get ideas for the use of this new sound in your backing-up.

EXERCISE XIV — MOVING UP THE NECK, USE OF "CHOKING"

Playing a melody break up the neck is really not very much different from playing down the neck. The patterns are essentially the same, and if you bear in mind certain principles that you learned from the exercises in rhythm and back-up, you'll have no difficulty. For example, full chords must be held with the left hand, the "Y" position should be used in most instances to accentuate the beauty of high notes.

Essentially, the banjo fingerboard can be divided into three parts. The first part lies between the nut and the 5th fret, and this is where you play the melody at the low position. The next portion lies between the 5th and the 12th fret, and the third portion lies above the 12th fret. Since the nut position and the barred position at the 12th fret are both G chords, the melody can be played exactly the same at these two positions, the only difference being that the high position gives a higher sound, of course. Fix a capo at the 12th fret and play "Cripple Creek" just as though you were playing it down at the nut, and you'll see what I mean. Although it is not a common practice to go into a melody break at this high position, it could be done by barring across with your index finger (at the 12th fret), then playing exactly the same as at the nut position, except for new fingering (your index finger is immobilized when barring, so you will have to give the other three fingers a real workout).

The middle position, between the 5th and 12th frets, offers a slightly different problem. When chording the G, you have to use the low C finger position, to make for easier maneuverability. You will see for yourself when you try playing at this position. There are many examples in the song section from the **"Foggy Mountain Banjo"** album, and the left-hand fingering is given above the tablature to aid you at this new position. Examples of this are seen in the 'Sallys' and in "Fireball Mail."

Choking is a technique by which a note is slurred by pushing the string to the side after plucking it. The slur is smooth, and the instant that the right hand plucks the string, the left hand starts to push (or rarely, pull) that string to the side. The slacker the strings are, the easier it is to accentuate a "choke," and therefore; most choking is done high on the neck, although occasional low position chokes are used.

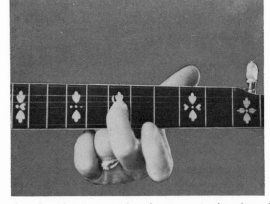

The actual musical mechanics involved are simple—a note is played, then the string is stretched mechanically, raising the note either one fret or even two frets, depending upon whether you want to raise the pitch a half tone or a whole tone. Examples of whole tone chokes can be heard in "Reuben," and in "Lonesome Road Blues." In this type of choke, in which there is no set pattern or speed, the middle finger of the left hand should do the choking, as it is the strongest. Whole tone chokes in "Lonesome Road Blues" are shown below:

A good half-tone choke to practice over and over is shown below:

The left hand, in the above pattern, uses this position:

     The choke is done by the little finger.

Another half-tone choke is used in a common ending lick:

The parentheses ( ) means that a note is optional.

An example of a low neck position in which a choke could be used is in the C⁷th chord in "Ground Speed":

Rarely is a choke achieved by pulling the string toward the palm, in order to stretch it. Such an example is in "Dig a Hole in the Meadow"—C Tuning, as played in the **"Carnegie Hall"** album:

Occasionally, a note is choked, held at its stretched position, then when that string is plucked again, it is immediately released, giving a choking, slurred tone in the opposite direction (the note is lowered):

An example of this can be heard in the back-up, in "Lonesome Road Blues."

Choking is an excellent way of "talking" with the banjo, particularly when the "Y" position is used. An example of this is "Mama Blues" on the **"Carnegie Hall"** album which is done in D tuning. Special "sound effects" can also be done this way. One is to choke two strings at once, getting a sound that imitates a train whistle:

In the above exercises I have demonstrated at least one or two ways of using the various rolls and licks described. There are many other variations and possibilities that haven't been shown, simply because of the impossibility of showing everything that can be done on the banjo in a book of any length. But I believe there is enough material here of all my styles of picking to enable you to understand how a lot of these variations are played, although they might not be explained in detail here.

In other words, there is still a lot of work left for you to do. Listen to all the records you can, go to shows and see musicians play in person whenever you can, and analyze their playing (as well as your own!). Practice with friends — there is no substitute for practice and experience and hard work. Set high standards for yourself, and don't be satisfied with less than your full potential. But above all, enjoy your banjo. Good Picking!

song

section

INDEX

FOGGY MOUNTAIN CHIMES

(G tuning)

EARL SCRUGGS

LITTLE DARLIN', PAL OF MINE

(G tuning)

A.P. CARTER

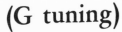

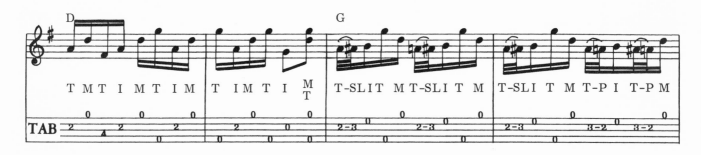
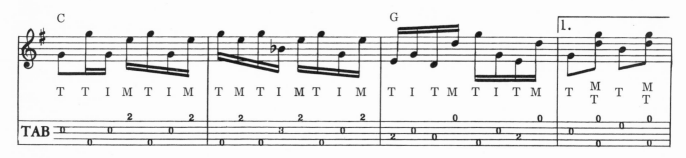

SALLY ANN

(G tuning)

84

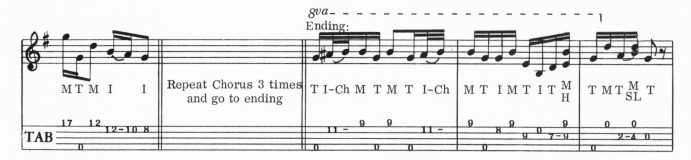

FOGGY MOUNTAIN BREAKDOWN

(Featured in the film "BONNIE AND CLYDE")

EARL SCRUGGS

(G tuning)

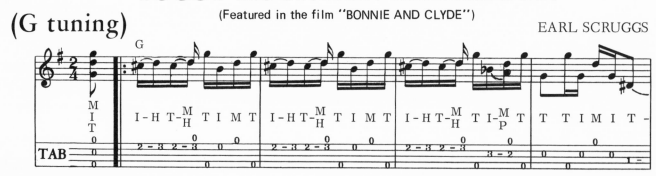

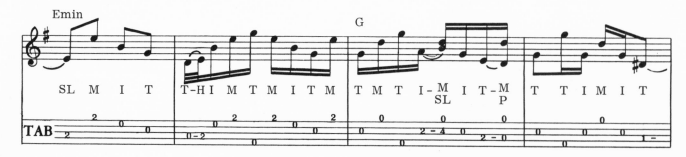

Copyright 1950 by Peer International Corporation
© Copyright 1962 by Peer International Corporation

YOU BAKE RIGHT WITH MARTHA WHITE
(Martha White Theme)

By Martha White Mills, Inc.

(G Tuning)

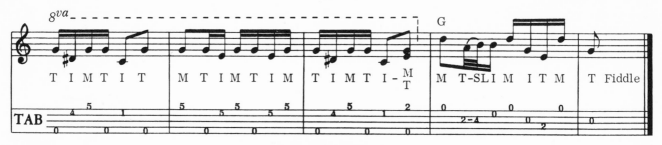

CRIPPLE CREEK

(G tuning, capo up 2 frets)

Arranged by Earl Scruggs

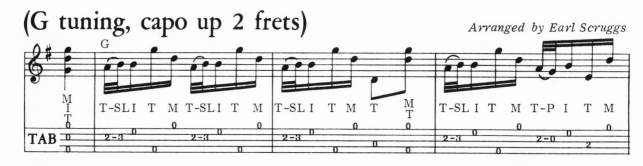

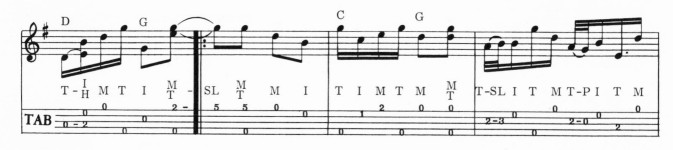

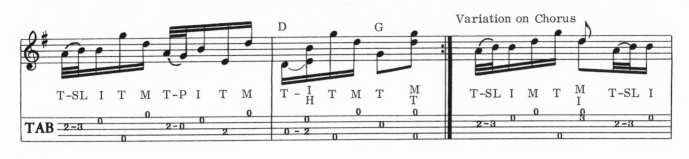

GROUND SPEED

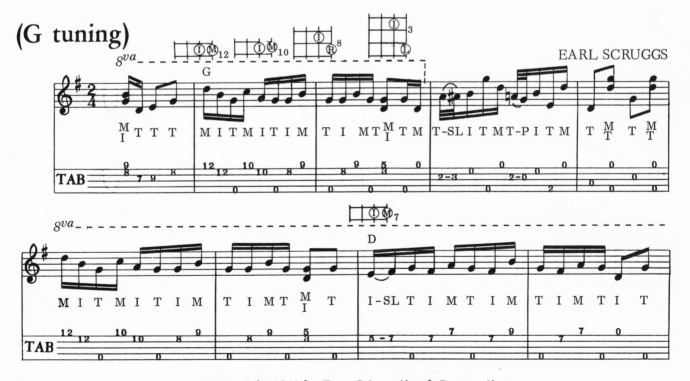

(G tuning)

EARL SCRUGGS

OLD FOLKS

(C tuning)

EARL SCRUGGS

HOME SWEET HOME

(C tuning)

Arranged by Earl Scruggs

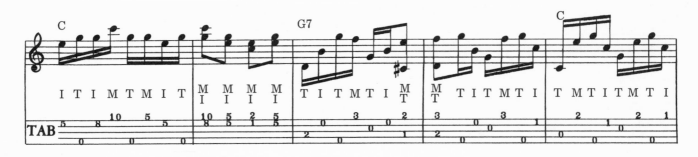

DOWN THE ROAD

(B-capo up 4 frets)

LESTER FLATT and EARL SCRUGGS

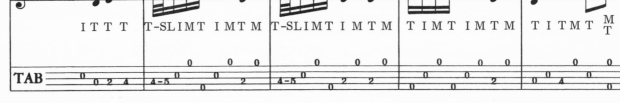

GROUND HOG

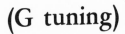

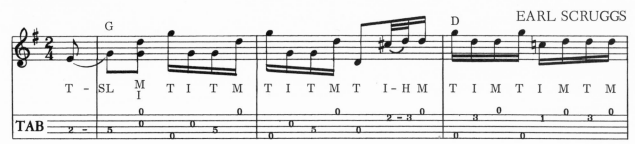

© Copyright 1968 by Peer International Corporation

CARELESS LOVE

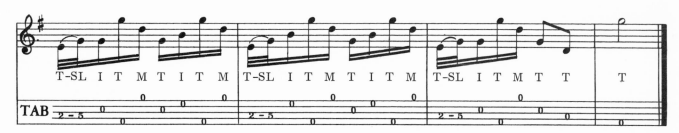

© Copyright 1968 by Peer International Corporation

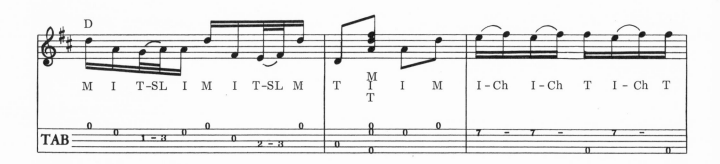

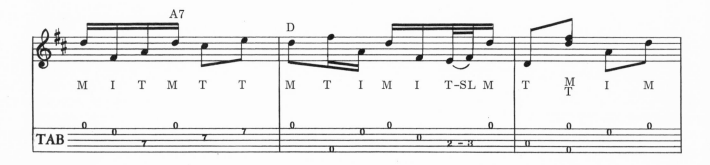

PRETTY POLLY

(G modal tuning)

Arranged by Earl Scruggs

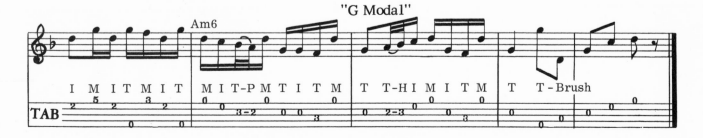

NASHVILLE BLUES

(D minor tuning)

EARL SCRUGGS

LONESOME ROAD BLUES

(G tuning)

This tune played one octave higher than written.

EARL SCRUGGS

JOHN HENRY

(D tuning)

EARL SCRUGGS

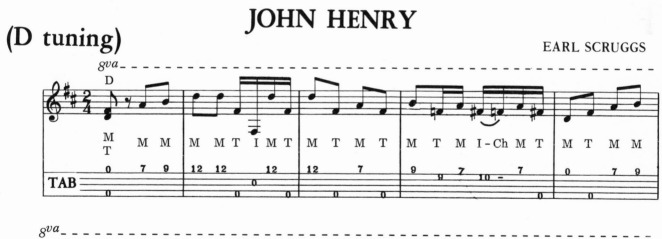

*Left hand fingering:

RANDY LYNN RAG

(G tuning)

EARL SCRUGGS

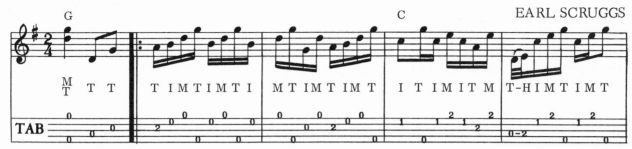

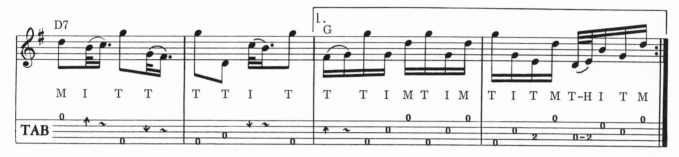

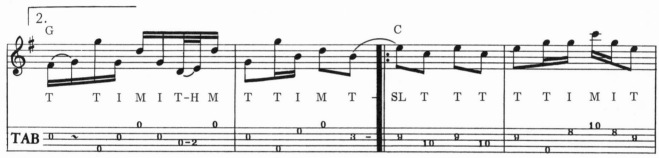

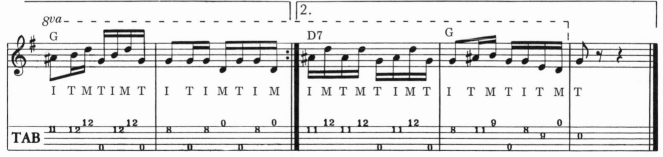

FLINT HILL SPECIAL

(G tuning)

EARL SCRUGGS

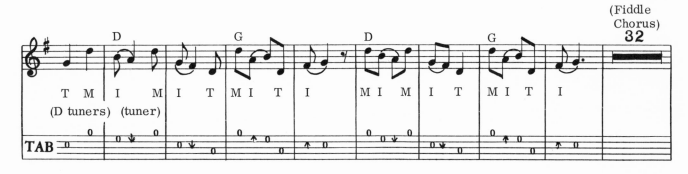

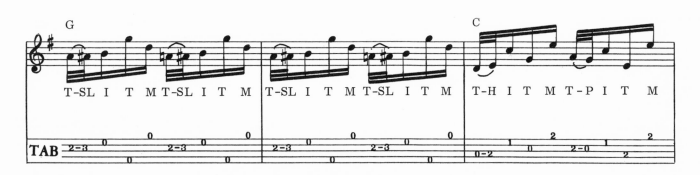

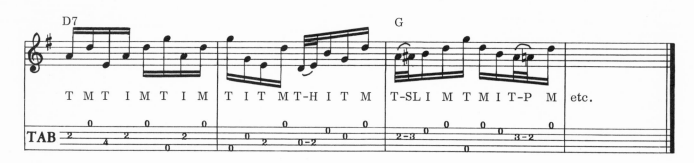

MAGGIE BLUES

(G tuning)

BUCK GRAVES, LESTER FLATT and EARL SCRUGGS

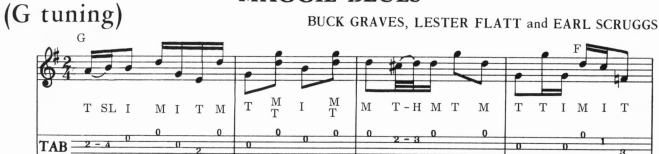

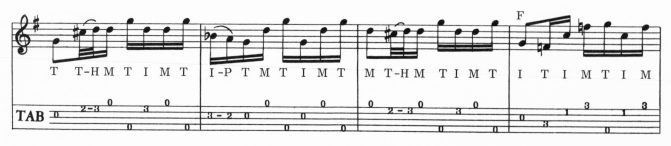

REUBEN

(D tuning)

EARL SCRUGGS

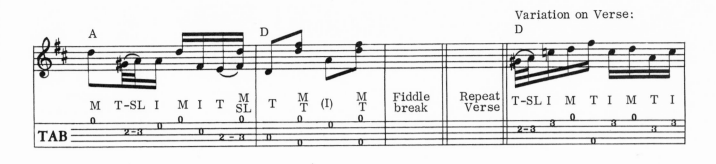

Variation on Verse:

Variation on Chorus:

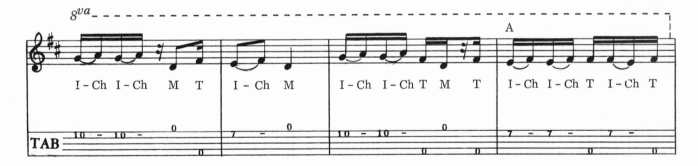

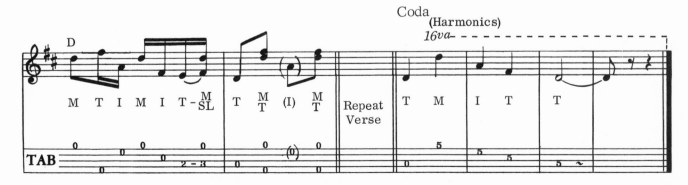

Coda
(Harmonics)

GOOD TIMES ARE PAST AND GONE

(A tuning)

LESTER FLATT and EARL SCRUGGS

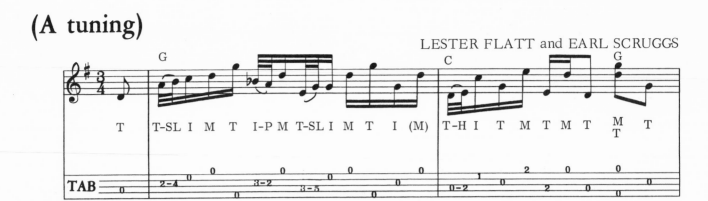

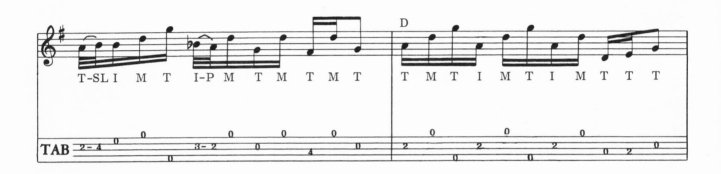

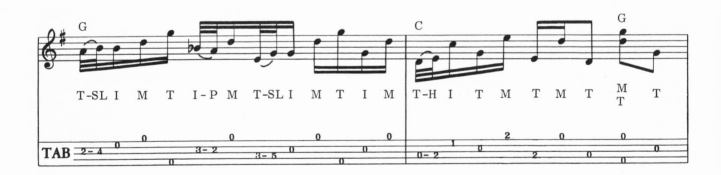

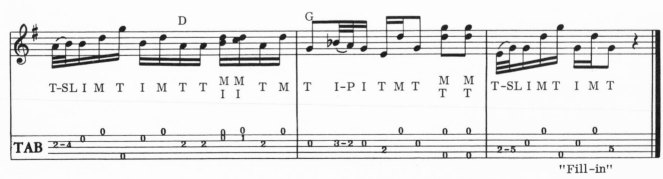

"Fill-in"

CUMBERLAND GAP

(G tuning)

EARL SCRUGGS

See ending of "Cripple Creek."

SALLY GOODWIN

Arranged by Earl Scruggs

(G tuning)

NINE POUND HAMMER

(G tuning)

Arranged by Louise Cirtain

112

DEAR OLD DIXIE

(G tuning)
This tune played one octave higher than written.

LESTER FLATT and EARL SCRUGGS

HOT CORN, COLD CORN

(G tuning)

AKEMAN, CIRTAIN and STACEY

EARL'S BREAKDOWN

(G tuning)

EARL SCRUGGS

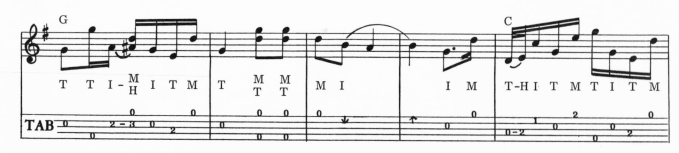

Copyright 1953 by Peer International Corporation
© Copyright 1968 by Peer International Corporation

116

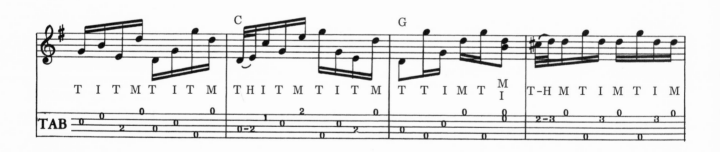

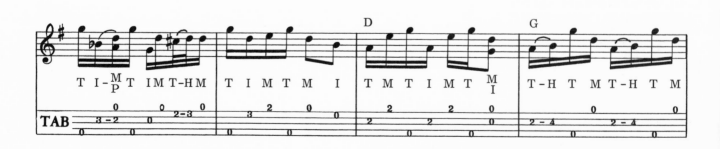

Ending:

SHUCKING THE CORN

(G tuning)

GRAVES, CIRTAIN and STACEY

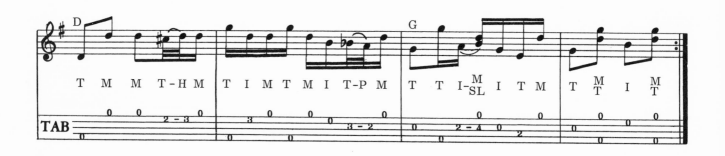

HOME SWEET HOME/SILVER BELLS
(Banjo Duet)

Arranged by Earl Scruggs

(C tuning)

HOME SWEET HOME

SILVER BELLS

The following songs are printed in three lines. The top (melody) line is the vocal part, the middle line is the banjo part showing the solo breaks in each recording, and the bottom line is the banjo tablature. If you listen to the recordings, you will see the relationship between the way the melody is sung and the way it is played on the banjo. Using the music as a guide, learn to play the banjo breaks, then compare your playing with what you hear on the recordings. — Try to duplicate the melodic emphasis and the rhythm that is achieved in the breaks as you hear them on the record.

THE BALLAD OF JED CLAMPETT

(G tuning)

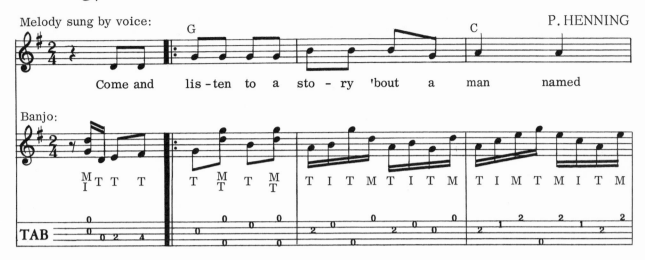

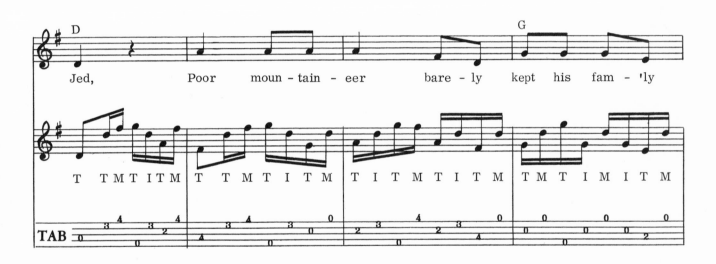

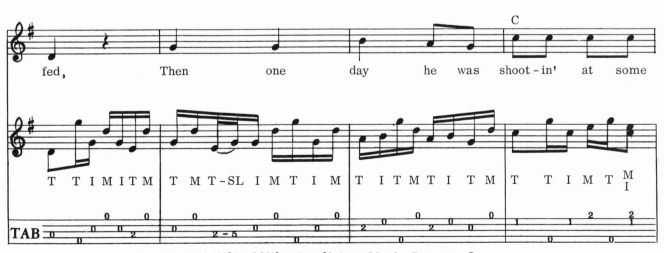

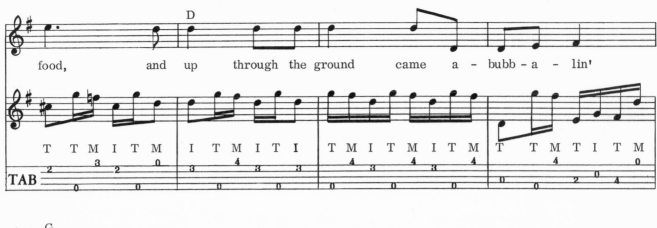

food, and up through the ground came a - bubb - a - lin'

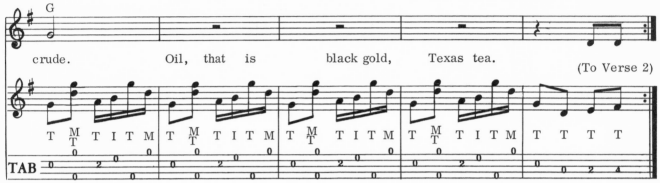

crude. Oil, that is black gold, Texas tea.

(To Verse 2)

(G tuning)

YOUR LOVE IS LIKE A FLOWER

E. LILLY, L. FLATT and E. SCRUGGS

Melody as sung:

It was long, long a - go in the moon-light, We were

Banjo plays:

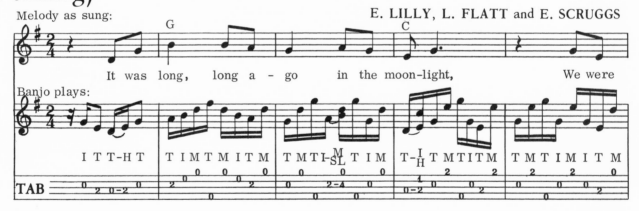

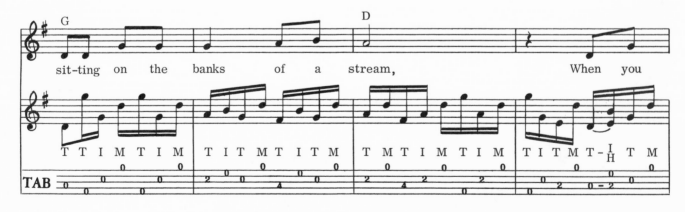

sit-ting on the banks of a stream, When you

whis - pered so sweet - ly "I love you,"   As the

wa - ters mur - mured a tune.

MY CABIN IN CAROLINE

(G tuning)

LESTER FLATT and EARL SCRUGGS

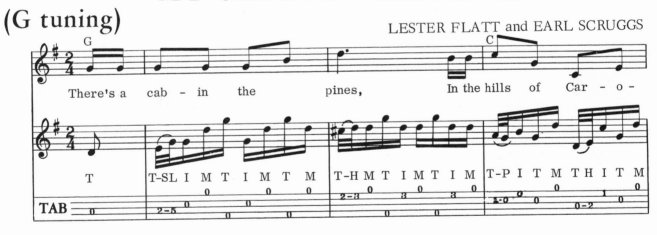

There's a cab - in the   pines,   In the hills of Car - o-

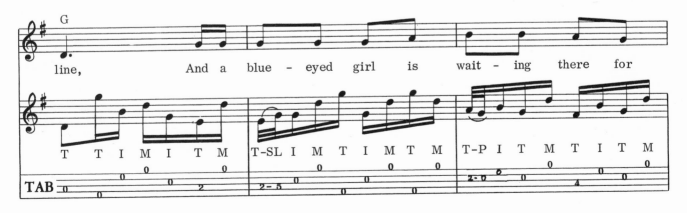

line,   And a blue - eyed girl is wait - ing there for

BLUE RIDGE CABIN HOME
(G tuning, capo up 2 frets)

CIRTAIN and STACEY

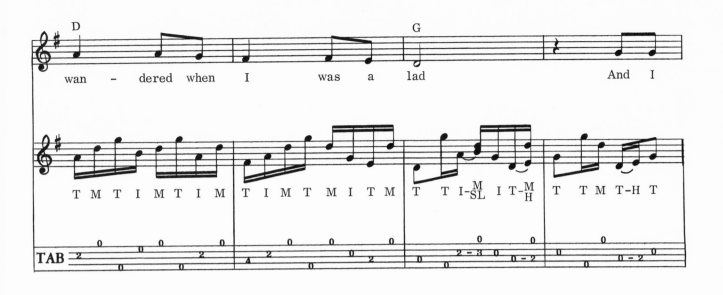

wan - dered when I was a lad   And I

T M T I M T I M   T I M T M I T M   T T I-SL I T-M/H   T T M T-H T

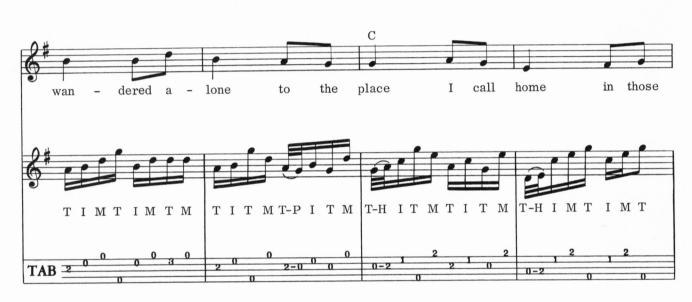

wan - dered a - lone   to   the place   I call   home   in those

T I M T I M T M   T I T M T-P I T M   T-H I T M T I T M   T-H I M T I M T

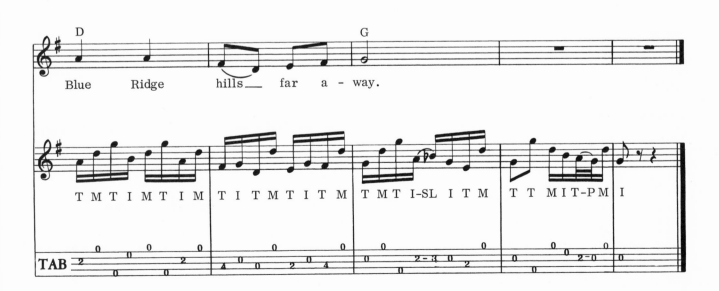

Blue   Ridge   hills__ far a - way.

T M T I M T I M   T I T M T I T M   T M T I-SL I T M   T T M I T-P M I

CHAPTER 12
How To Build A Banjo

by Burt Brent, M.D.

To fully understand your banjo, you should become familiar with its construction. A banjo is a unique instrument, in that there are many variables in its construction and parts which can affect the tone and the ease in which the instrument can be played.

Many automobile owners are dependent upon their favorite mechanic for every little thing that goes wrong with their car, as they only know how to turn a key, step on the gas, or hit the brake. A repair or adjustment is costly, as well as inconvenient. The exact same principles apply to the banjo. If you understand the "anatomy and physiology" of the instrument—in other words, its construction and mechanism of its parts, you will appreciate the instrument and respect it, as well as saving yourself the expense and inconvenience of leaving it at a music shop for weeks or months at a time. There is also much self-satisfaction in being able to make these repairs and adjustments yourself.

This, then, is the main importance of this article. Secondarily, it will teach you inlaying, fancy decorative type instrument work, gold-plating, etc., if you care to try some for yourself, as most banjo players do at one time or another.

BUILDING A BANJO NECK

Unfortunately, the art of decorative musical instrument making has been lost through the evolution of our modern mass production age, but there are still many musicians that desire the old-time, artful instruments. It is for this reason that I have compiled these articles on inlaying, neck, and decorative shell-building, so that you may have an instrument suited to your taste. The techniques described are partly mine, but they mainly have been passed down to me by friends with the same interest.

Many serious banjo players, at one time or another, get the urge to make their own banjo neck, or to try some inlaying of mother-of-pearl. There are two main problems that will confront you, if you have such desires; first, learning certain tricks and short cuts that make it quite easy to

do, and second, finding out where to buy the necessary materials and equipment. This article will try to provide the necessary information.

WOODS

The best wood, in that it is hard and has a beautiful pattern to its grain, is curly maple. Unfortunately, there are several drawbacks. First, this wood tends to warp and twist unless it is properly seasoned and kiln-dried. (Be sure to specify the above requirements when ordering.) Second, it is difficult to obtain a piece that is large enough. Other woods that are good to use are the various hard maples, birdseye maple (if you want an unusual pattern), walnut, and mahogany.

GLUING THE BLOCK

I advise laminating the neck, as well as setting a steel rod or bar, to prevent warpage. However, you may have a piece of curly maple large enough to make a neck, and won't want to spoil the curly pattern with laminations.

The best glue to use is weldwood resorcinol glue, available in large hardware stores. Use as many clamps, wood vices, etc. as are available to get sufficient pressure for perfect jointing. The temperature of the room and clamping pressure time is specified on the glue container.

An attractive laminating pattern to try is shown below:

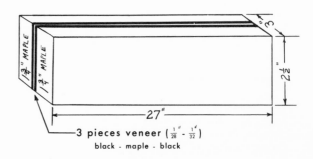

Fig. 1

Then, planing the top and being sure that it is perfectly flat, laminate it in the same manner:

Fig. 2

Incidentally, black and colored veneers are available under the name of "rainbow veneers." You may want to incorporate other colors besides black into your banjo. Beware of gaudiness however. Some old banjos had green and orange veneers and I would recommend looking at one before attempting the use of bright colors. You may like it, or you may not.

Next, draw the following pattern on the side of the block using a straight-edge where possible:

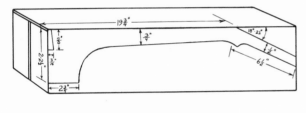

Fig. 3

Heel height varies with the height of your shell.

The notch for the tension hoop will have to be carefully cut and fitted to your banjo, but approximate dimensions are supplied.

CUTTING OUT THE ROUGH SHAPE

Using a band saw, make the following cuts:

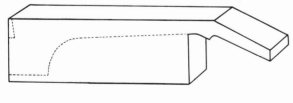

Fig. 4

Leave the block as shown above, so the peghead may be worked on with the advantages which will be explained later.

LAMINATING THE PEGHEAD

Glue the same three veneers on top of the peghead so it looks like this:

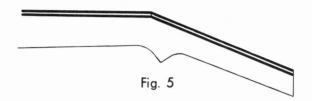

Fig. 5

In gluing veneers like this, use a ½ or ¾ inch board above and below the peghead with a layer of waxed paper between the boards and peghead. The reason for this is to avoid gluing them to the peghead, as with pressure, glue will be forced through the veneer. Using this technique allows for even gluing pressure to veneers:

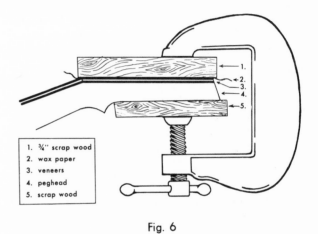

1. ¾" scrap wood
2. wax paper
3. veneers
4. peghead
5. scrap wood

Fig. 6

SETTING STEEL BARS AND RODS

The easiest strengthening method is the use of steel bars. Hardware stores carry them, and the standard size is 3/16″ x ½″. Also available are L-shaped bars. Using two of them together, a T-bar is formed.

Borrow a router from someone, or, using one at a woodshop, cut a groove in the block exactly the same size as the bar. This groove will extend into the peghead where the bar will have to be cut flush (giving strength to the peghead). The groove in the peghead will later be hidden with another piece of veneer. If a T-bar is to be used, adjust the level of the router bit and make several more cuts.

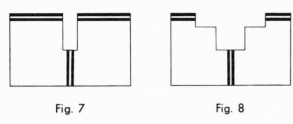

| Fig. 7 | Fig. 8 |

ROUTING THE BLOCK FOR STRAIGHT AND T-BARS

Inserting the two L-bars to make a T-bar, glue them in with a strong epoxy glue (again, available at most hardware stores). (See (Fig. 9)

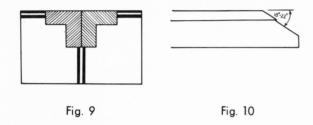

| Fig. 9 | Fig. 10 |

Refer to Fig. 29 at this time to get a preview of a cross-section of the finished neck.

The end of the bar will have to be cut at the same peghead angle in order to fit flush. (See Fig. 10) The bar should not extend all the way into the heel, but should be 1½″ shy of the end of the heel. (Fig. 11) Fill the space in front of it with wood. This allows for the attachment of the neck to the shell:

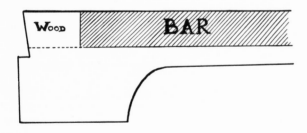

Fig. 11

SETTING AN ADJUSTABLE ROD

Some people prefer to put in an adjustable rod, so that possible bowing of the neck can be corrected.

In most hardware stores you can obtain the ⅛″ threaded rods that you need. Put a slight bend on one end, and weld a washer and nut in place on the end. Then, after routing the groove, set in neck **without glue:**

Fig. 12   ADJUSTABLE ROD

A slot will have to be cut for the washer to fit into. This holds the rod when tension adjustment is made at the opposite end.

An Allen nut is at the peghead end and is adjustable by the use of a wrench. A plate will have to be put over the peghead to hide this nut and groove.

PREPARING THE PEGHEAD AND FINGERBOARD

Next, glue a piece of veneer on the top of the peghead to hide the routed grooves. This veneer should match the wood used in the fingerboard. A hardwood should be used, and ebony is the hardest and prettiest for this purpose. If an adjustable rod is used, leave a ⅝″ x 1″ opening in the peghead, which will later be covered by a plate:

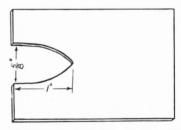

Fig. 13

When the fingerboard is glued on, it should be ⅛″ from the end of the block, to allow a place for the nut:

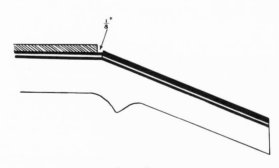

Fig. 14

MAKING THE FINGERBOARD

Using a 3/16" piece of ebony or rose- wood, cut out the pattern and sand the edges straight and smooth, using sandpaper attached to a hand sander. The pattern can be traced from a good banjo, or if one is not available, the following pattern can be used:

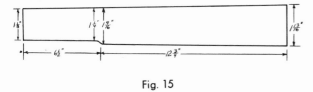

Fig. 15

Glue this fingerboard on **very carefully, centering** both ends over the groove for the bar. Remember, the end near the peghead should be ⅛" from the end of the block, allowing a place to set the nut. (See Fig. 14, 16). A white glue should be used for this.

Use a board and waxed paper again to obtain adequate pressure and don't use too much glue this time. After clamping, wipe off all excess glue that oozes between the fingerboard and block, or else it will be difficult to remove after it is dried and gluing of the ivoroid binding will be difficult.

Use white glue for the above operation, because being water soluble, it can be steamed and the fingerboard removed if this ever becomes necessary.

After this is dry, you must determine that your fingerboard is flat. Lay it on a perfectly flat formica counter or other surface and check. If it is not **perfect,** now is the time to correct it by the following methods:

Glue construction-type sandpaper of a medium grade onto a **flat** wood surface (it may require several pieces of sandpaper). Now turn the block upside down so that the fingerboard rests on the sandpaper. Run the block back and forth, occasionally checking the fingerboard against the perfectly flat surface you have chosen and repeat the process until you are satisfied that your fingerboard is perfectly flat.

CUTTING FRET SLOTS

There are several methods of tracing out the fret patterns. Copy a good standard banjo pattern, or design the pattern yourself by the following method:

The distance from the nut to the bridge is called a scale. Measure this distance, multiply it by 1/17.835 and the resulting figure will be the distance at which the first fret is placed from the nut.

Now measure the new scale (distance between bridge and 1st fret) multiply it also by 1/17.835. This will give you the distance at which the second fret is placed from the 1st, and so on, for all the frets. In other words, the chromatic scale at which frets are placed is a decreasing logarithmic progression of 1/17.835. Draw the lines on the fingerboard with a pencil. To insure perfectly perpendicular lines, use a T-Square.

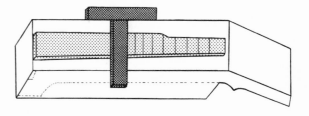

Fig. 16

The best method I can think of for cutting perpendicular slots of uniform depth is by the following method:

Purchase a guitar-makers saw or a similar saw blade. The blade is 1" x 5", and is very fine. Using this saw blade, make the following set-up:

1. Cut two pieces of hardwood ¼" x 1" x 10".
2. Drill holes through the wood pieces and blade, then fasten them together with bolts and nuts. Cut off the excess bolt, so that the blade is protruding below the wood by ⅜".

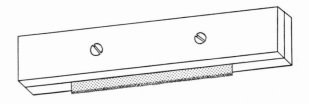

Fig. 17

3. Make two wood clamps using ¼" x 1" x 5" hardwood with perfectly straight edges. Use bolts and wing-nuts:

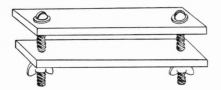

Fig. 18

4. **To cut a groove** (fret slot).
   a. place one clamp over the block and tighten when its edge is lined up with the pencil marked fret.
   b. place the other clamp on and slide it next to the tightened clamp.
   c. drop the saw blade into the slot between the clamps.
   d. tighten the other clamp.
   e. gripping the wood ends of the saw, slide it back and forth (cutting the groove) until the wood of the saw rests against the wood clamps, as illustrated.

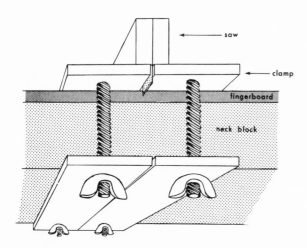

Fig. 19

Your groove will be ⅛" deep and perfectly straight, cut perpendicular to the surface of the fingerboard.

Incidentally, the block should be placed in a wood vice while sawing for stability and for free use of both hands on the saw.

Frets are available from most instrument repair shops or banjo companies.

The slot you just cut may not be wide enough to set a fret. If not, the grooves can easily be widened by a few strokes from the proper sized coping saw blade. Experiment on a scrap of wood to be sure of the right size blade. The fret should go in fairly easily upon hammering. If the slot is not wide enough, the fret won't go in. If it is too wide, the fret will slip out and white glue must be applied to hold it in place.

Do not put the frets in at this time, however, as it is necessary to first put in your inlays (also at a later time). Also, the frets would get nicked during shaping of the neck if you put them in now.

CUTTING OUT THE PEGHEAD

Next, cut out the peghead shape, using a bandsaw. The block, resting flat on the bandsaw table, will allow the same bevel to be cut on the entire peghead. Be sure that the peghead base is slightly wider than the fingerboard, to allow for the ivoroid binding on the fingerboard to make the neck and peghead of equal widths at their junction. (See Fig. 21)

My favorite peghead shape is the old mastertone fiddle shape, shown in the photo below. You may want to design your own shape, however.

Now, with the fingerboard pointing up, cut out the neck, allowing an ⅛″ margin around the fingerboard where the binding will fit in, as shown in Fig. 21. Again, use the bandsaw:

Fig. 21

Then, glue the same three veneer laminations to the bottom of the heel for decoration.

Now, shape the banjo neck with rasp files. Again, it is advisable to put the neck in a vice while working on it. **Don't** clamp onto the fingerboard!

THE HEEL

Before shaping the heel, make a heel plate with the following pattern:

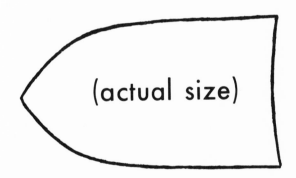

(actual size)

Fig. 22

HEEL PLATE

Cut the heel plate out of the same type wood as the fingerboard, ⅛″ thick. Bind it with ivoroid binding.

Method for binding is as follows:
1. Cut an appropriate sized piece of binding off the strip, then dip it into hot water for a few seconds until it begins to curl.
2. Quickly apply it to the side of the "heel plate" and hold till it cools. You can bend the binding while it's warm until you are satisfied that the shape is nearly correct.

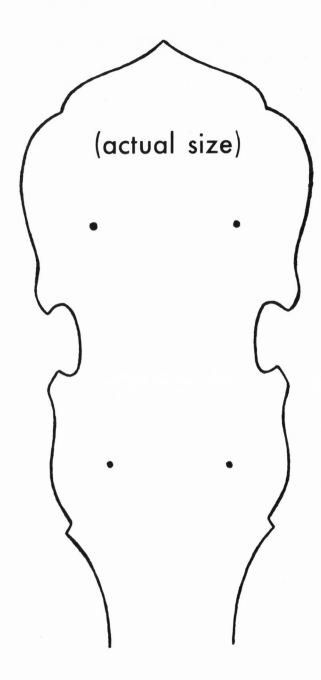

(actual size)

Fig. 20

MASTERTONE FIDDLE-SHAPED PEGHEAD

CUTTING THE BANJO NECK SHAPE

Next, lay the block on its side, and finish cutting out the neck shape, including the notch for the tension hoop. (Use a bandsaw.)

3. Glue it on with household cement. When dry, sand the edges flush with the wood.

Now, trace this heel plate pattern on the bottom of the banjo neck (Fig. 23). Using your files, shape the heel up to your pencil mark. Do not glue the heel plate on at this time:

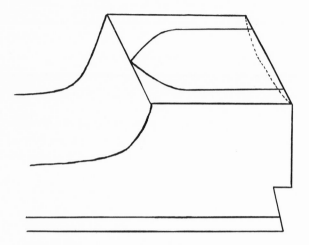

Fig. 23

Incidentally, the peghead can be bound in the same manner described for the heel, but it is a tedious job and it is difficult to cut the peghead out of veneers.

The neck will now have to be fitted to the shell.

From above, cut the neck in the same curve as the shell, using a bandsaw. (See Fig. 23)

Then use a file to round the inside of the neck attachment so that it fits the shell at the proper angle (3°). To determine when you have the right angle, tape a straightedge across the fingerboard, hold it to the shell and note that the protruding yardstick should be about ⅜" above the drumhead where the bridge is (about 7" from the attachment of the neck):

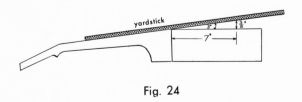

Fig. 24

Round the part of the neck in the notch that fits against the tension hoop, so that the whole neck fits tightly against the shell and tension hoop.

At the same time, note that a straight line down the middle of the neck **must** bisect the head equally. Determine this with a straightedge. If it is not centered, trim neck attachment with a file until the correction is made:

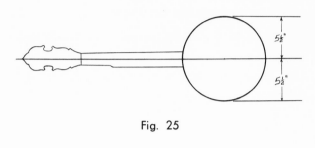

Fig. 25

HOW TO ATTACH THE NECK AND HEEL PLATE

Before gluing the heel plate on, drill two ¼" holes into the neck for two threaded rods which can fit into these holes. Then drill a hole down through the heel through the two rods, but **not** through the fingerboard. Through this hole place a ⅛" screw:

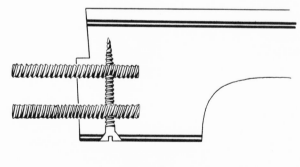

Fig. 26

The neck can be attached to the shell with two large hexagonal nuts. Be sure that the two rods are far enough apart so that the hexagonal nuts can be turned and tightened!

The heel plate can now be glued on.

FITTING THE PEGS

Drill the holes carefully into the peghead, using an electric drill. It is best to have the pegs beforehand to insure correct fitting.

A non-slip 5th string peg with a setscrew is the best standard non-mechanical 5th peg which still looks conventional and traditional. The hole should be drilled under the 4th fret, centered in the side of the neck. Tap it (purchase a tap at your hardware store with the same size threads as the threads found on your fifth string peg). Now, the threads of the peg will screw in without splitting the neck. Remove the pegs after fitting them, so that they don't interfere with finishing.

INLAYING MOTHER-OF-PEARL

You can make your own inlays, or else buy pre-cut inlays.

To make your own inlays, you need flat sheets of pearl (which you can grind out of abalone shells, or purchase).

Make your own inlays by cutting them out with a jeweler's saw, and filing with a small set of "needle files," while the pearl is held by a small vice.

INLAYING TECHNIQUE

Practice on a scrap piece of wood before trying to inlay an instrument.

Design your whole fingerboard pattern on paper before you start inlaying.

1. Make the inlay (or use pre-cut inlays).
2. Center it between the fret slots.
3. Trace its outline with a fine pencil sharpened with sandpaper. Another fine tracing method is:

   a. fasten the inlay to the fingerboard with a drop of contact cement.
   b. spray the wood with a fine coat of shellac.
   c. blow a sprinkle of talcum from your hand across the still tacky shellac, let it dry for a minute.
   d. remove the inlay, and a perfect outline remains.

4. Routing the wood to the same size and depth of the inlay may be done with a small scalpel and fine chisels, but this is difficult for ebony inlaying. Far superior is the use of a small hi-speed electric drill which has a variety of uses. If you are working with ebony, buy several carbide bits which can be purchased from a dental supply company. They will not burn out as fast as others do.

5. After routing the space for your inlay and fitting it, glue it in place by the following method:

   a. make a pile of fine sawdust of the same type wood into which you are inlaying by sanding down a scrap of that wood into a box.
   b. mix some of the sawdust with a small amount of white glue.
   c. fill the space with this mixture, then press the inlay into it, allowing the mixture to ooze up through any spaces. Be sure that you don't set the inlay below the surface of the fingerboard.
   d. allow to dry for 24 hours, then sand flush with a fine sandpaper or emery paper, sanding lengthwise along the fingerboard.
   e. if an inlay is to cover several fret spaces, cut it into its respective pieces, rather than leave it whole, so that the fret may be hammered in without breaking the inlay. (Fig. 27)

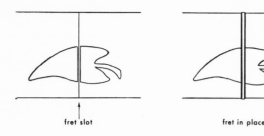

fret slot   fret in place

Fig. 27

Fancy vines can be inlaid by using pewter or 1/16″ copper wire for the vine, pearl for the leaves.

The method below discloses how I inlaid the vine in the photograph.

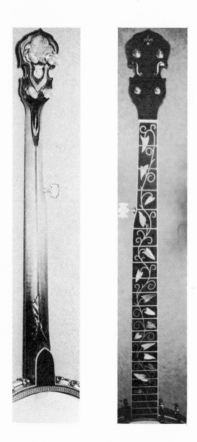

1. Cover the slotted fingerboard with two layers of masking tape.
2. Draw the lines on the masking tape with pencil where the frets are located.
3. Trace the inlays with fine pencil on the tape.
4. Draw the vine.
5. Using a fine scalpel, cut along the pencil lines, then peel the tape leaves or flowers off. Trace around the vine, cutting a double line wide enough for the pewter wire. Peel this out, using a pin.

6. Now the whole thing can be sandblasted to the proper depth. (The sand bounces off the tape, but erodes the wood.)

The results are fine, and only a minimal amount of trimming with your high-speed drill will be necessary to fit the inlays into place.

As you make your inlays, and while the fingerboard is being blasted, be careful to keep the inlays in order and not misplaced. I have found an easy way to do this: simply fasten several strips of masking tape to a board, sticky side up. Stick your inlays to the tape, in order, as you make them. The fret spaces can be labelled on the tape to further simplify matters.

7. The tips of the vine's tendrils should be filed to a point before inlaying.
8. An example of this type of inlaying is seen in the photograph of a neck I recently made. Other fingerboards are shown in photographs to give you ideas of what has been or can be done.

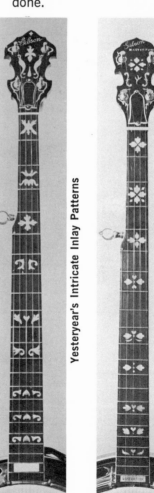

Yesteryear's Intricate Inlay Patterns

Variation of Above

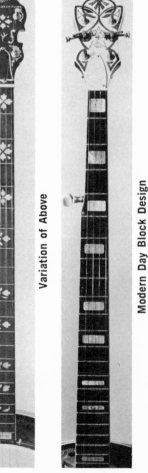

Modern Day Block Design

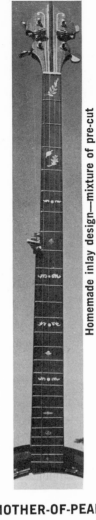

A Banjo that belonged to Uncle Dave Macon

Homemade inlay design—mixture of pre-cut purchased inlays, and hand-cut inlays.

Pearl and Abalone vine, unfretted fingerboard

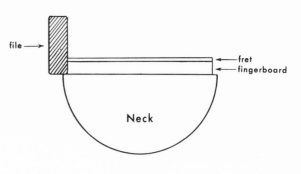

Fig. 28

ENGRAVING MOTHER-OF-PEARL

Engraving veins into pearl leaves in your vines, initials, etc., can be attractive, and is fairly easy to do. Obtain a "graver," (a small sharp steel knife-like tool) from a jeweler supply, and practice on scrap pieces of pearl. After inscribing the pearl, which is done with a smooth, firm stroke, rub black jeweler's wax across the pearl and wipe off the excess. Only the engraved depressions will remain black.

SETTING THE FRETS

1. Cover the head of your hammer with several layers of masking tape to cushion it and to prevent nicking the frets.
2. Tap the frets into place, clipping them off evenly at the edges of the fingerboard, using a wire-cutter.
3. When they are all placed and clipped, run a metal file in the groove where the ivoroid binding will go, as shown in Fig. 28. This will leave the frets flush with the fingerboard.

BINDING

Now glue the ivoroid binding in the groove by the same method described for the heel plate. The neck can now be sanded smoothly, going from medium to fine grade sandpaper.

OTHER FANCY IDEAS FOR YOUR BANJO NECK CARVING THE HEEL

Carving a heel such as the one in the photograph, is not difficult.

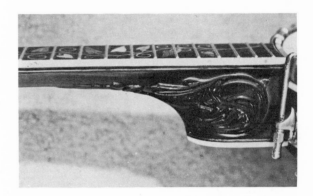

Draw the pattern on paper cut it out, then pin it on the neck. Trace it with a pencil, then turn the paper around, pin it to the other side and trace it there. Then use your scalpels and chisels to carve. Several examples of carving are shown in photographs to stimulate your imagination.

POSITION DOTS IN THE BINDING

Drill small holes in the binding at the required positions (1, 3, 5, 7, 10, 12, 15, 17, 19, 22). Fill the holes with a mixture of white glue and ebony dust. The result will be black position dots.

Another technique is to inlay abalone dots in the binding as shown in the photograph.

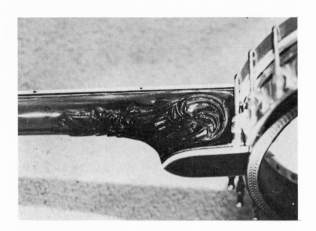

This will test your patience, as they are difficult to cut out of pearl. Run a hand sander obliquely across the edges of the fingerboard, thus beveling it and the frets:

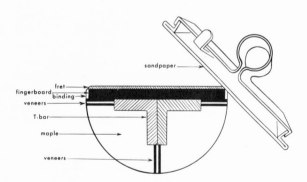

Fig. 29   CROSS-SECTION OF THE NECK —
beveling with a hand-sander

LAMINATING THE PEGHEAD

The undersurface of the peghead can be beautifully laminated. Do this before you begin to round the neck. I attempted this and the results can be seen in the photograph.

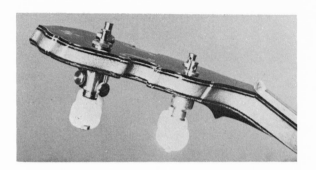

After the neck is finished, place the nut, made of bone, (bought at any stringed instrument shop) with a drop of white glue after shaping it. The string grooves should be cut with a 3-cornered file.

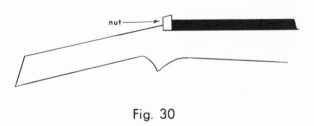

Fig. 30

5th string nuts and hooks can be obtained from various manufacturers. A screw can be substituted for a 5th string nut, but is unsightly.

FINISHING THE NECK

A good finish on the neck is important. In addition to adding beauty to the instrument, it protects the wood and also allows you to slide your hand back and forth smoothly and rapidly while playing.

Preliminary Work:

1. Sand with fine sandpaper, fill all cracks with wood filler, cover fingerboard with masking tape.
2. "Washing" — dampen a rag with lacquer thinner, go over the neck once.
3. Spray (do not use brush!) 2 or more coats of clear lacquer on the neck, until the grain is filled. Wait until the lacquer is ¾ dry before spraying each additional coat. Under normal drying conditions this will be about 15-20 minutes.
4. You are now ready to apply one of four types of finishes; solid, opalescent, clear, or sunburst.

Solid Finish:

1. After completing above steps, spray solid color of your choice (opaque lacquer). The number of coats of this solid lacquer depends on how many defects, blemishes, etc., that have to be covered.
2. When ¾ dry, spray 3 or 4 coats of clear lacquer at regular intervals.
3. Wait 24 hours to insure thorough drying.
4. Using wet emery paper, "water-sand" the "orange-peel" (uneven surface) effect off of the lacquered surface of the neck to get a perfectly smooth surface.
5. Spray two more coats of clear lacquer at regular intervals.
6. Wait 24 hours.
7. "Compounding"—use a fine abrasive compound. Rub the neck with the compound, using a cloth, until a glass finish is obtained—the "orange-peel" effect will disappear.
8. "Waxing"—wax the neck using a fine wax.

Opalescent Finish:

1. Repeat preliminary work steps through "step 3—spray" two coats or more of clear lacquer before tinting process.
2. The opalescent tint—mix clear lacquer 50-50 with lacquer thinner.
3. Add and mix oil stain (cherry or mahogany oil stain). Necessary proportions—2 oz. stain to one pint lacquer-thinner mixture.
4. Spray the opalescent tint you have mixed on to the neck, according to how much you want to tint the wood. (The less you

spray, the more the grain of the wood will show through).
5. Repeat the rest of the process as for solid finish (begin with step 2).

Clear Finish:

Same as above, except—eliminate the opalescent tinting with the oil stain.

Sunburst:

1. The same process is used as for the other finishing methods, except that "sunbursting" is substituted for the spraying of solid or opalescent tint.
2. Sunburst types
   a. Oblong—for necks
   b. Circular—for guitar bodies, banjo resonators
3. Process
   a. spray yellow stain in middle (neck or body)
   b. use opalescent tint mix of various mixtures—1½ oz., 2 oz., 2½ oz. stain to one pint lacquer and spray from center toward the periphery, using the thicker (and darker) mixtures toward the periphery, finally ending up with a black stain.
4. A general finishing hint is to keep lacquer buildup to a minimum to prevent cracking.

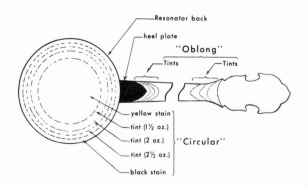

Fig. 31   SUNBURST FINISHING

GOLD-PLATING

The finishing touch to a fancy instrument, in many artists' and musicians' eyes, is gold-plating of the metal parts. To have this done commercially is costly, but you can actually plate your small metal parts (brackets, pegs, etc.) on your kitchen stove.

Purchase some gold-plating solution and some zinc rods from a dental supply company and obtain a small pyrex bowl. The solution can be used over and over, so one pint goes a long way.

Remove the grease, fingerprints, etc. from the object to be plated by immersing in a weak acid medium, or a safer method around the home is to warm some water with a small amount of baking soda and detergent and cleanse the object, then dry it without touching it again. Three minutes or so will do the job. Heat the gold solution on your stove in the pyrex bowl until vapor begins to rise from it. Drop the object into the solution and touch the zinc rod to it. In about 3-5 minutes the object will be beautifully plated.

BUILDING A DECORATIVE BANJO SHELL

Using Weldwood resorcinol glue, glue and clamp together layers of various fancy hardwoods until a block 1' X 1' X 2" is formed. I made the following block, shown in the illustration:

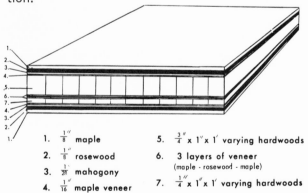

1. $\frac{1}{8}''$ maple
2. $\frac{1}{8}''$ rosewood
3. $\frac{1}{28}''$ mahogony
4. $\frac{1}{16}''$ maple veneer
5. $\frac{3}{4}''$ x 1" x 1' varying hardwoods
6. 3 layers of veneer (maple - rosewood - maple)
7. $\frac{1}{4}''$ x 1" x 1' varying hardwoods

Fig. 32 CONSTRUCTION OF THE BLOCK

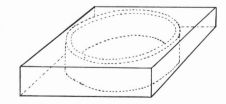

Fig. 33 CUTTING OUT THE SHELL

All the layers are 1' X 1' boards of varying thicknesses (1/28", 1/16", ⅛", ¼", ¾"). The layers with the squares (¾" and ¼") consist of 1" X 1' strips of various fancy hardwoods (12 of them constitute a layer that will be 1' X 1').

In clamping there is one problem: getting pressure from the sides, in order to form solid joints between these 1" strips. It may be accomplished by the following method:

1. The bottom layer (⅛" maple) should be 14" X 12", whereas all other layers are 12" X 12".
2. Screw down a strip of ¾" X 1⅞" X 12" hardwood on both ends of the bottom layer of 12" X 14" maple, as shown in the illustration below. (Fig. 34)
3. Glue all the layers together in order. The 1" X 1' strips must be covered with glue on all four sides. Use a large paint brush to apply the glue, as the block must be glued together rapidly. The brush should be washed out with water, before the glue dries.
4. Using clamps and sheets of waxpaper and scrap plywood (1' X 1' X ¾") for vertical pressure (as described in peghead veneer portion of the banjo neck chapter), apply the partial vertical pressure needed (don't tighten the clamps all the way at this time).
5. There will be ¼" between the hardwood strips screwed to the bottom maple layer, and the rest of the block. To exert the horizontal pressure necessary for firm joints between the 1" strips, simply hammer in triangular wooden wedges, as shown in the illustration below. Then the clamps exerting vertical pressure can be further tightened.

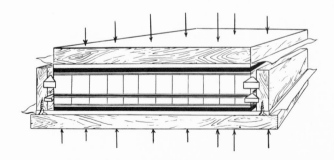

Fig. 34 GLUING THE BLOCK

When this is completely dry, remove the clamps, and using a bandsaw, cut off the excess of the bottom layer of maple, its ¾" strips and the wedges—you now have a 1' X 1' X 2" block.

Dry this block in your oven (with just the pilot light on) for several days, then let it sit around in a dry room for a week or more (as long as your patience holds out) to insure thorough drying.

CUTTING OUT THE SHELL (See Fig. 33)

1. Draw two lines across the block (from corner to corner) to find the center point.
2. Using a compass, draw an 11¼" diameter circle on the block.
3. I was taught to make the outside cut with a router, as well as the inside cut, but since the outside is for show, I have found a quicker and easier method for clean results:

   Cut out this circle with a bandsaw. Then mount the circular block on a lathe baseplate. Put this on a wood lathe, and using a **sharp** straight lathe tool, cut a straight smooth edge. While it is still spinning on the lathe, use several grades of sandpaper to get a very fine finish. The final diameter of this block should now be 11".
4. If you have a tone ring to fit on the shell, cut the necessary notch in the block, while it is still on the lathe, using the straight sharp lathe tool, so that the side of the tone ring and shell are flush, as shown in the diagram below.

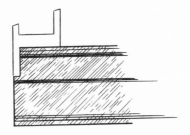

Fig. 35   FITTING THE TONE RING —

cross section of the block
and an arch-top tone ring

5. Remove from the lathe and unscrew the baseplate from the round block.
6. Using a router, set the radius at 4⅞", then cut the inside diameter out. (This will leave the shell thickness at ⅝".) You probably won't be able to get a router bit long-

er than 1¼", so the best way to accomplish this is to drill a tiny hole through the block at the center point, using a drill-press, in order to help find the exact center on the other side. After routing a circle on one side, turn the block over, and rout a circle on the other side. You now have a shell ⅝" thick. Don't throw the rest of that block away! It makes a beautiful bowl when turned out on a lathe. Here's what the finished shell will look like.

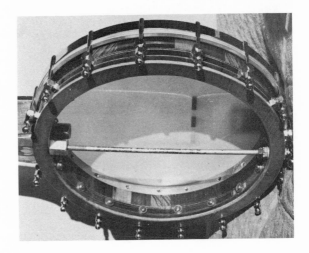

FINISHING THE SHELL:

Purchase a set of bracket holders and brackets, and drill the appropriate holes in the shell through which the bracket holders can be fastened with ¾" bolts. Also, at this time, the holes for the neck attachment should be drilled into the shell.

Then fine sand the shell, and finish as described in neck finishing. Use a clear finish.

CHAPTER 13

How To Make Your Own Scruggs Pegs
(Cam Type)

Outlined below is a simple method of making your own Scruggs Tuners which will work reasonably well. The cost of materials is minimal, but you will need an available electric tool workshop, and a good deal of your time.

1. MATERIALS NEEDED.

a. 6" length of ½" x ¼" hard steel, available at most hardware stores.
b. two plain banjo pegs.
c. several "taps" also available at your hardware store. The sizes needed are: 4 x 40, 5/64" to match bolt.
d. two Lionel train transformer knobs.
e. two small bolts, size 5/64".
f. two threaded bolt pieces, size 4 x 40.

2. PROCEDURE.

Read these plans carefully before beginning, as once you begin to drill your peghead, there's no turning back.

a. using a hacksaw, cut out of hard steel the rough shape of the cam.

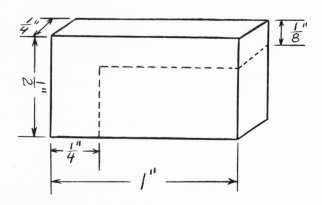

b. trim with metal files,

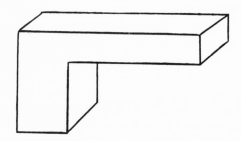

c. round the end,

d. drill a series of holes through the top of the cam,

e. using "needle files" connect the holes, making a slot,

f. shape the tip, for decoration, with the resulting cam:

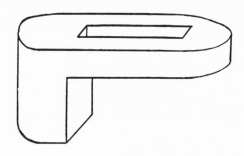

g. screw a 4 x 40 bolt into a Lionel train transformer knob, (which has 4 x 36 threads) so that the bolt jams and stays fixed in knob.

h. using a 4 x 40 tap, tap the string hole of the peg, so that the bolt turns through it freely.

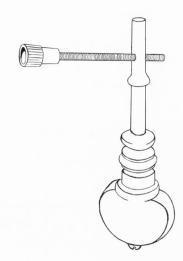

i. drill a 5/64″ hole into the top of the peg (drill down about 3/16″). Use a vice and an electric drill press. Tap this hole to fit a tiny hexagonal bolt as illustrated (it should be about 5/16″ long.)

j. screw the cam down to the peg, using the hexagonal bolt. Screw the other bolt through the peg until it rests against the cam (mark the exact spot).

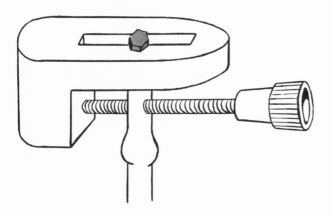

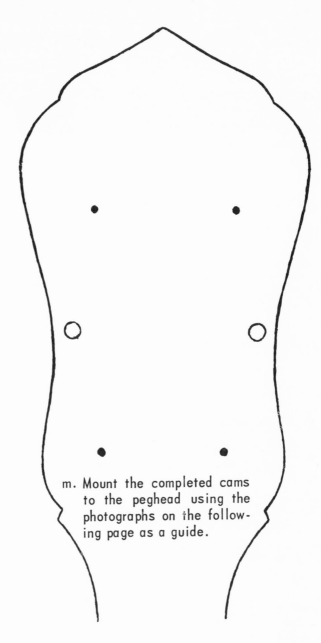

m. Mount the completed cams to the peghead using the photographs on the following page as a guide.

k. drill a hole into the cam, at that spot, which should just go into the cam about (1/16″ - 3/32″).

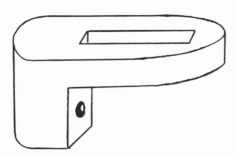

l. drill holes in the peghead, centered between the other pegs (1, 2) (3, 4) and as far to the sides of the peghead as possible.

n. without the cams touching the strings, put the banjo in D tuning. Swing each cam, so that they push out the 2nd and 3rd strings, meeting them exactly perpendicularly; then, by turning the terminal knobs, tune the banjo into G (the 2nd string tunes up 2 frets, the 3rd up one fret). Now set 2 headless nails as shown in the diagram, which act as stops (drill holes first, so as not to split the peghead.) Swing the cams back off the strings (you're now back to D tuning) and place two more nails as shown in the diagram. This keeps the cam from swinging all the way around when in D. The nails must be lower than the strings, or else they will stop the strings as they are stretched by the cams.

NOTE THE DIAGRAM. Actually, the second set of nails could be set, so that the cams are still touching the strings when they are in the lowered position. This lack of "dead travel space" will improve the action of your cams.

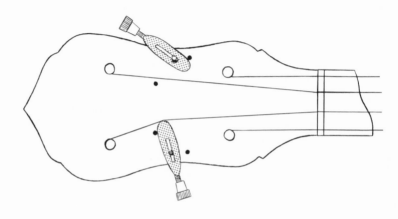

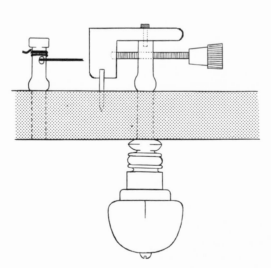

This article shows you the mechanics of making one type of tuner. There are many improvements that can be made. Let your imagination work for you, trying pulleys to reduce friction, etc., and don't limit yourself to one way of doing things. Experimenting and creativity will not only enhance your mechanical ability, but will also enrich your playing style and ability.

Earl Scruggs — Biographical Notes

For several years, I have wanted to write a book about the banjo. Over a period of about eight years, and consulting with a number of people of different talents, this book was made possible.

It has been my desire throughout my years of picking the banjo to get others interested in the instrument. Needless to say, I would like to share the knowledge I have gained about the banjo and I hope this book will fulfill the purpose for which it was intended.

I have been asked many times about how I became interested in the banjo and how I went about learning to play the way I do. I thought it might be of interest to write a short history of my childhood days and the fine banjo pickers I had the privilege of knowing as I grew up.

I was raised in a musical atmosphere of the fiddle, banjo, guitar, autoharp, etc. I have two brothers and three sisters and all our family played stringed instruments except my mother and youngest sister, Venie Mae. My father, George Elam Scruggs, played the fiddle and the banjo. My older brothers, Junie and Horace, and my two older sisters, Eula Mae and Ruby, played the banjo and guitar. My mother, Lula Ruppe Scruggs, played the organ. Probably no other family enjoyed music and singing more than we did. My brothers and sisters could pick a few hours and seem to forget it more easily than me. But the banjo stayed in my mind most of the time, if I was playing with friends or working on the farm.

Homeplace

My father died when I was four years old. Due to his eight month illness prior to his death, I never remembered his picking although I do remember him.

Lula Ruppe Scruggs   **George Elam Scruggs**

My brother Junie started playing the banjo in 1927. By 1930, he was referred to as just about the best and, in many people's opinion, the best banjo player around. He played a very good three-finger style and what I remember best was the way he could play the melody and at the same time keep a good even beat going, whether he was just picking alone or had a guitar accompaniment.

There were several three-finger banjo pickers I admired who lived near our Flint Hill community. There was Mack Woolbright, a blind banjo picker who recorded with Charlie Parker on the Columbia label in the late 20's. I remember him from a visit he made to my Uncle Sidney Ruppe's home; rocking in a rocking chair and picking "Home Sweet Home" in the key of C. The G⁷ chord he played in this number was one of the most thrilling sounds I had ever heard. At this time I was about six years old and I wondered how a blind person could play so beautifully.

Other banjo players who lived near us were Leaborn A. Rogers, Rex Brooks, DeWitt "Snuffy" Jenkins, Smith Hammett, and Mack Crow.

The one who inspired more people at that time was probably Smith Hammett. (As far as I can trace it back, he was the first banjo player to use three-finger picking.) Smith's wife, Mrs. Ola Hammett, and my mother were cousins. Even though transportation was a problem, we visited them or they visited us quite frequently. I was not only fascinated by Smith's banjo playing, but also by a little banjo he owned. This banjo had approximately a nine inch head and the neck was about half the length of a standard banjo. It gave me a thrill to pick this banjo because I could hold it in my lap and be able to reach the chord positions.

Smith and Ola Hammett

John Ross, fiddle
Smith Hammett, banjo
Brooker Self, jug

Smith Hammett was born on February 21, 1887 at Gaffney, South Carolina. He was the son of Martin and Missouri Hammett. He married Ola Harriss, February 24, 1907. They raised nine children — one son, Howard, was killed in New Guinea on June 24, 1944. Smith was raised in a musical family. His father played the fiddle and two of his brothers also played musical instruments. Smith took up playing as he grew up and could play almost any kind of an instrument, fiddle, organ, etc. He was killed on February 1, 1930.

My brother, Junie, was one of the people influenced by Smith's playing. Junie said, "The desire to learn to play came to me one morning about 1:30 A.M. Smith had come by our house from a dance and Mom and Dad fixed him a snack. He started playing the banjo, I woke up and thought that was the prettiest music I had ever heard. I made up my mind then to play the banjo and the more I heard of a banjo the more eager I was to learn to play one. Smith showed me three chords and from that I learned to play."

I also enjoyed listening to Fisher Hendley from WIS in Columbia, South Carolina. He was with a group who called themselves "The Aristocratic Pigs." This name was derived from their sponsor, which was a meat product, and their advertising slogan was "our meats come from aristocratic pigs." Fisher was the emcee and had a band that played music with a touch of Western atmosphere to it. However, two or three times during the week, he would play a number on his banjo, along with the fiddle player. To me, this made the listening really worthwhile. ("Snuffy" Jenkins informed me that Fisher Hendley died in March, 1964. He had moved to Venice, Florida, where he was managing a motel).

A sound that I was to hear later in the 30's and 40's was that played by "Snuffy" DeWitt Jenkins and his three-finger style. I listened to him on Radio Station WIS in Columbia, South Carolina, and to watch him play was a special treat. He is also a very fine comedian. ("Snuffy" is still living in Columbia and every time we work a show there, we impose on him to play a number on stage with us. However, the audience will never let him off stage with just one tune).

"Snuffy" Jenkins

"Snuffy" was born in October, 1908 in Harris, North Carolina, the youngest in a family of ten, all of whom except the parents were musical. "Snuffy" started playing the fiddle when he was very young. Being too small to use the bow, he recalled, "I picked it like a mandolin. Soon after that I took up playing the guitar with my brother. In 1927, we started playing with two fellows who both played a three-finger style of banjo. Their names were Smith Hammett and Rex Brooks. This is when I started playing my style of banjo in Cleveland County, North Carolina."

"Snuffy" settled in Columbia, South Carolina in 1937 and joined a string band to play on Radio

Station WIS. "Snuffy" is the only one of the original group left. The group was given the name, "The Hired Hands" in 1948 upon the death of Byron Parker, who was generally known as "The Old Hired Hand."

I asked "Snuffy" to write some history on his musical career and he told me the following: "When I was playing the guitar I found it too hard to fret. So, along came Smith Hammett and Rex Brooks playing our style and it sounded so good I couldn't stand it. Smith was killed in 1930, and Rex died in a car wreck about the same time. We were playing for dances and Fiddler's Conventions at that time. Later, in 1936, the job came open with J. E. Mainer and I joined him for about five months. We joined Byron Parker, "The Old Hired Hand," in April, 1937. We first got to traveling about a hundred miles on trips, and I thought if the world was as big in the other direction as it was that way, it was a whopper!"

("Snuffy" has a Folk-Lyric album released, titled, "Carolina Bluegrass," — "Snuffy" Jenkins and the Hired Hands.)

Earl Scruggs, banjo
Horace Scruggs, guitar

My brother, Horace and I used to spend many happy hours picking away on the banjo and guitar. The combination of the two worked out very well. We would pick on rainy days when we couldn't work on the farm, and especially on winter nights after we had studied our school lessons.

The only way I could pick Junie's banjo, or the old one my father played, was to sit on the floor with the body part of the banjo to my right and slide it around quite a bit, depending on what position on the neck I was attempting to play.

Horace Scruggs, guitar
Earl Scruggs, banjo

This was pretty rough on a banjo, so Junie wasn't too pleased when he would catch me playing his. He had a very good banjo in those days even though he had only paid around $17.00 for it from a mail order company. When I was around the age of ten, I kept his banjo almost full time since he had married and was too busy farming and raising a family to play it very much.

I didn't have a banjo of my own until I was thirteen years old. I purchased one for $10.95,

and I will never forget the aroma that came out of that new banjo when I opened the case. I used this banjo until 1941, and then bought a better one in a pawn shop. At this time, a great number of banjos could be found in pawn shops in North and South Carolina and could be purchased at prices from $25.00 to $90.00, depending on how long they had been hanging in the pawn shops. These were the old model Mastertones and Whyte Ladyes. These banjos would be considered a bargain today at prices from $500.00 to $1,000.00.

My first picking before an audience was at a local Fiddler's Convention. I walked, banjo around my back, occasionally picking a bit as I went along from our farm in the Flint Hill community to Boiling Springs, North Carolina where the contest was held. (A number I later wrote and recorded, "Flint Hill Special," was named for the community where I grew up. It is located approximately six miles from Shelby, North Carolina. The community had a two-room school, a church and a grocery store). At that

"My Student days at Flinthill"

time I was too excited about the convention to remember all the banjo players who entered the contest but I do remember Leaborn Rogers and "Snuffy" Jenkins were there. A first, second, and third prize was given to the best band, banjo picker, etc., and three people judged the contest. I played "Cripple Creek" and won either first or second prize. (This was probably due to my young age, and I also later learned this number was a favorite of a couple of the judges).

When I was around the age of six, Junie was playing one or two nights each week for square dances near where we lived. I played guitar for him one night and soon after that we played on Radio Station WSPA in Spartanburg, South Carolina. If I recall correctly, I think my other brother, Horace played on the station with us.

When I was eleven, I played again on the station in Spartanburg with Horace and T. W. Bryant. This was a talent show that came on at 7:00 A.M. I recall that T. W.'s father drove us to Spartanburg in his rumble-seat Model T Ford. We left home that morning at 3:00 A.M. This was all very exciting and we arrived in plenty of time for the broadcast. (This was twenty-four miles from where we lived).

There was an employee from Lily Mills in Shelby who built a small recreation building on Broad River near where we lived. His purpose was to rent the building out for Fish Fry's, or to officials at the mill who wanted to use it for parties.

There was space for thirty or forty couples to dance. Here is where I started making money. He would pay me $3.00 and plenty of hot cat fish and hush-puppies to pick for a couple of hours, which usually ran into three or four. This was good experience and I enjoyed it, although it became tiring picking alone. At that time there were no amplifiers around, in fact, no electricity within three miles of the place.

A radio station in Gastonia, North Carolina started having local groups play on Saturday morning programs. When I was fifteen, I played with a group called the "Carolina Wildcats." I worked with this group for eleven months. It was fun to arrive at the station and read the fan mail. (It usually consisted of letters from our relatives). We always rehearsed on Thursday or Friday night, depending on the obligations of the members of the group.

On Saturday nights I would usually pick with Dennis Butler who played an excellent old time fiddle. We would sometimes play at some friends' home until after midnight just for experience. And the word experience really fits in; most of the time, Marvin White would accompany us on the guitar. This was a great help to me in learning to play back-up and occasionally take the lead break on the banjo.

In 1939, I worked a short time with Wiley, George, and Zeke Morris on WSPA in Spartanburg, South Carolina. The program was sponsored by a cross-tie company and their program was on during the winter months when the farmers were free from their crops and could listen to the radio. The program was broadcast from 6:00 to 7:00 A.M. This was a thrilling stage of my life because I was working with real professionals.

Earl Scruggs, fiddle   Horace Scruggs, guitar

Junie Scruggs, banjo

In the early 40's, when the war came along, I left the farm and got a job at the Lily Mills in Shelby to help support my mother and younger sister, Venie Mae. My work week usually consisted of seventy-two hours because, at that time, it was difficult to get help for the mills. During that time, I didn't do much playing away from home, but occasionally someone would come by our house and want to pick a few numbers.

I continued on the seventy-two hour work each week until my doctor advised me to take off a week to rest. I had always wanted to spend some time in the mountains so I went to Asheville, North Carolina for a week. While I was there I met a group that was playing on a noon show on WWNC. They invited me to play with them during the week and of course I accepted the opportunity.

I stayed on at the mill until the war ended in 1945. I had decided I wanted to make music my career. I went to Knoxville, Tennessee and was hired by "Lost" John Miller. After working with him for two weeks in Knoxville, he started a morning radio program on WSM in Nashville on Saturday mornings. I worked with him for three months until he decided to stop full time road work.

In December, 1945, I went to work in Bill Monroe's group, in which Lester Flatt was working as the lead singer and guitarist.

I stayed in the group until February, 1948. I had become rather discouraged with show business and decided to move back to North Carolina. I also felt it would be better for me financially to live with my mother in Shelby and find work locally. However, two weeks after I left the group, Lester quit too. We decided to try to organize a group and work around the Carolina area. We organized the group, worked on a station in Danville, Virginia for a couple of weeks and then moved our location to Hickory, North Carolina.

"Lester and Earl"

Quite a number of artists work under a tremendous amount of strain and pressure while they are performing. Lester seems to have a built in system of blocking away from his mind any strain whatsoever, as far as the audience can detect. I have worked with him almost daily since 1945, and I personally feel he works under very little strain. His speaking is most appealing and sincere and he has a selling drive to his voice. The depth and body of his voice gives him a singing talent that is unsurpassed.

It was during the time that we were working in Hickory that I married the former Louise Cirtain whom I had met in Nashville in 1946. We were married on April 18, 1948 in Gaffney, South Carolina. Louise is the only child of Ewing and Mamie Elizabeth Cirtain, and she is originally from Grant, Tennessee, a small community forty-five miles East of Nashville. She, too, grew up admiring old time music. Her grandfather had one of the first radios in the community and all the neighbors would gather in on Saturday nights to listen to the Grand Ole Opry, or the WLS Barndance. Louise worked as a bookkeeper prior to our marriage. She has been business and booking manager for the Flatt and Scruggs Show since 1956.

We stayed in Hickory about a month and, due to financial reasons, decided that wasn't the place for us. For example, one date we worked was in a small theatre, booked on a percentage, with the cost of advertising coming off the top. Our grand total take for the night was seventeen cents each. We went to Bristol, Virginia for an audition on WCYB and was accepted on the station.

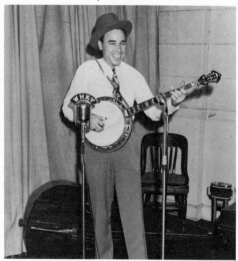

Our first group consisted of Howard (Cedric Rainwater) Watts, Jim Shumate, Lester and me. Mac Wiseman joined the group during the time we were working in Hickory, North Carolina.

Cedric played the bass fiddle and was the comedian in the group. He could sing virtually any part of a song but he was used mainly as a bass singer in the group. Jim Shumate played the fiddle, and Mac Wiseman was a guitarist and tenor singer.

The name our group was tagged with was "Foggy Mountain Boys." This name originated from the theme song we were using when we first organized. The song was an old Carter Family number "Foggy Mountain Top," which we used for some time.

Earl Scruggs, Cedric Rainwater, Jim Shumate
and Lester Flatt

Later, when we began singing commercials as a theme, the "Foggy Mountain Top" was dropped but the name has remained with the group.

Shortly after we started our radio programs in Bristol, we were asked to sign a recording contract with Mercury Records. We recorded our first session in the summer of 1948 in Knoxville, Tennessee. The four sides consisted of "God Loves His Children," "I'm Going To Make Heaven My Home," "We'll Meet Again Sweetheart," and "Cabin In Caroline." During the period between 1948 and 1950, we recorded twenty-nine sides for Mercury. These have all been released in three LP's by Mercury. Our first session for Columbia was recorded on November 21, 1950, and we have remained with Columbia Records since that time.

We worked on WCYB in Bristol until March, 1949. During the period between 1949 and 1953, we moved around quite frequently. We worked on radio stations in Knoxville, Tennessee; Lexington, Kentucky; Roanoke, Virginia; Tampa, Florida; Raleigh, North Carolina and back to Knoxville in the fall of '52. When we returned to Knoxville we were working a noon radio program and then driving out within 150 miles of Knoxville each night for personal appearances. It was during some of these appearances that Mr. Efford Burke, one of Martha White Mills salesmen, attended our show. He mentioned our group to Mr. Cohen Williams, President of Martha White. Mr. Williams came to Knoxville, saw one of our shows and asked us if we would be interested in working their radio programs on WSM in Nashville. We accepted the offer and came to Nashville on the first of June, 1953. Since that time we have been sponsored continuously by Martha White Mills on radio and television.

During 1953 and 1954, we were not on the Grand Ole Opry. We were only working seven radio shows each week on W.S.M. for Martha White Mills. These shows were broadcast Monday through Friday at 5:45 to 6:00 A.M., and on Saturday evening, a radio show from W.S.M. studios and on Sunday morning an all hymn program. Working personal appearances each night and doing all the radio programs live were getting the best of us. In September, 1954, our sponsor agreed to let us tape the radio shows, and, at that time, we accepted an offer to work on the Saturday Night Barndance show in Richmond, Virginia. We also worked two daily noon radio shows in Crewe, Virginia, and taped our Martha White and WSM daily radio shows from there. We were also taping a daily show for WRVA in Richmond which gave us a total amount of four 15 minute radio shows each day, and then worked on the barndance on Saturday evenings. We continued making a personal appearance at a school, theatre, or stadium almost every night in the week.

While we were working at the station in Richmond, the cast was scheduled to go into New York City for a two week engagement at the 48th Street Theatre. This was the first time our music had been heard in that area and the audiences were very enthusiastic over it. (Reviews were favorable with the exception of one critic. Her review said, "Whoever heard of hillbillies on Broadway.")

We returned to Nashville in January of 1955, Martha White had expanded into several areas and we began working television shows for them six days a week. Our weekly circuit took us from Columbus, Georgia; Atlanta, Georgia; Florence, South Carolina; Huntington, West Virginia; Jack-

son, Tennessee and back to Nashville for a show on Saturday evening. This involved twenty-five hundred miles each week since the shows were presented live.

The only tragic incident that has happened to me since I have been in show business was a car accident on October 2, 1955. My brother had phoned me that my mother was in the hospital and had suffered a stroke. Louise, Gary, Randy and I were on our way to Shelby, and just out of Knoxville, a car ran out into the highway in front of us. The children were not injured but Louise and I stayed in the hospital for almost a month and I was off the road for a total of eight months. My mother died while we were in the hospital. I had both hips dislocated and a broken pelvis bone. I have had two operations since then as a result of the accident.

My doctor kept warning me that I should take care of my hip and not make any tiring trips. I decided I would learn to fly and this would eliminate so much traveling time on some of our long road trips. I started taking flying lessons in 1958 and bought a plane. I obtained a single and multi-engine instrument license, and whenever it is possible, I either fly commercially, or use my plane on personal appearance dates.

"First TV network appearance"
Photo: Tom Allen

The first national exposure our group had on television was in 1960 when we appeared on the Revlon Revue — "Folk Sound, U.S.A." This was followed by an appearance at the Newport Folk Festival in 1960; I had appeared at the 1959 festival without the other members of our group. We have also appeared on several network shows, "The Ernie Ford Show," "Jimmy Dean Show," "Tonight Show," Frank McGee's "Here and Now," "Les Crane Show," and, most recently, "The Beverly Hillbillies Show."

Guest appearance on The Beverly Hillbillies Show

Our group plays the theme music for the Beverly Hillbillies CBS-TV series. Mr. Paul Henning, writer and creator of the Beverly Hillbillies network show, attended four of our performances when we were appearing in Los Angeles prior to the time the show went on television. He liked the sound of our music and later asked us to play the theme for the series.

At Carnegie Hall

Louise and I have three sons, Gary, Randy and Stevie. All three seem to have developed a talent for music. Stevie is a little too young to start playing an instrument, but he can listen to a record and pick out particular runs that he likes. Gary plays a twelve-string guitar and has been taking music lessons for the past five years. He also plays the trumpet in the Madison High School band. Randy has been interested in playing an autoharp for the past three years and he has appeared on several of our television programs. He, too, is taking trumpet lessons at school and is presently learning to play the guitar.

Earl, Stevie, Gary & Randy

I would like to add hints and information on banjo playing. When I first began playing the banjo, I used the thumb and index finger. This is referred to as two-finger picking. However, I found that my rhythm was choppy and not as syncopated as I wanted it to be. My three-finger style of picking began when I was around the age of ten. I recall that my brother and I had gotten into an argument and I took my banjo and went into a room by myself. I was picking away, and suddenly discovered I was using the thumb, index, and middle finger rather than the usual two. The number I was playing at the time was "Reuben." For an entire week I played that tune and nothing else. I kept playing it over and over in order to become accustomed to using the middle finger on the notes. Soon after that, I was able to use the same technique on other songs.

At the time I first began playing the three-finger style, I still wasn't completely happy with the sound I was getting because the way I was picking didn't sound exactly like the other three-finger banjo pickers I had admired so much. However, I was very careful with my picking and learned later the style was much more versatile than the style I had previously been using. I could play slower songs as well as the faster tunes.

My dear old mother must have had nerves of steel and a built-in system of not hearing the noise because she never discouraged me about my playing. I do recall that one time when I was picking some kind of wild banjo runs she said to me, "If you are going to play, then play so the tune can be recognized."

I now realize how right she was, and I am a firm believer that the melody should be played so as to be recognized over the other picking. For this reason, I prefer to pick the melody notes as much as possible with my thumb since it is most capable of bringing out the strong melody notes.

I went through several stages during the years when I was learning to play the banjo. One was

a tendency to become disgusted with my banjo playing. Then, I also went through a stage of trying to play any tune I heard. I soon realized that every tune can't be played on the banjo. You may be able to accompany someone else very nicely, or accompany yourself when you sing, but you may have to leave out a banjo solo on some numbers. I would also like to mention that it is best to not become alarmed if you sometimes become disgusted with your playing. (If you do reach this point, lay your banjo aside for awhile and perhaps when you pick it up again you may find you have come up with a new idea.) This is normal and your progress may come in small bits but you will have quite a bit of knowledge adding up.

Looking back over my childhood days, I can't remember anything more satisfying and more pleasurable than the banjo. I remember looking forward to getting up early to build a fire in the fireplace and in our wood cook stove, just to sit before it and pick a few numbers before it was time to go to school or to work on the farm.

Some days I might be picking away on a song and some new run or pattern might spring up. Then, sometimes, I would go for several days and seemed to be at a complete stand-still as far as my playing was concerned. This may sound slightly unbelievable but I have actually dreamed about a certain run or a tune and I could get up the next morning and play it all the way through even though I had never played the song before. Occasionally, I would hear some other artist play or sing a song and I could adapt portions of that into my work.

In the late 30's and early 40's, I was greatly inspired by Roy Acuff and his Smoky Mountain Boys. Roy has carried a very professional show all down through the years. The act of Rachel and Oswald really gave me many enjoyable moments. They worked mainly as a comedy, brother and sister act and both of them played a fine old time frail 5 string banjo. Oswald was the first person I remember to do such fine work with the old un-amplified steel Hawaiian guitar. His solo playing was outstanding and he had a number of great fill-in licks he used when he was backing Roy's solo parts. I don't suppose his tenor singing with Roy has ever been topped, as well as his solo singing on such a song as "Well, I Am A Going Down The Road Feeling Bad."

There were other groups who also inspired me and I suppose every musician has been similarly inspired by various groups.

One of my favorite people I had occasion to work with while I was on the Grand Ole Opry in the 40's was Uncle Dave Macon. There was probably never a musician before and chances are none since who enjoyed entertaining people more than Uncle Dave. In my travels with him, I remember a few goodies with which I was impressed. With all his fame and the money he made on shows, he never got away from his earthy or simple way of living. Fame, I think, is an understatement in his case, because it was my first experience of seeing a man so well loved by so many. People would walk, ride horse-back, you name it, just to see him perform, and I don't think he ever let them down. His slogan was, "I don't put on, I put out," and this he did. He didn't have an interest in a fancy or a society way of living, and he didn't try to impress anyone with his hotel address or fancy dinners.

He never ceased to drop a bit of enjoyment whenever possible. Due to his age and running the risk of taking a cold, he would ride at night in the automobile with a cap tied around his head. He never ate a meal without using a bib to protect his clothing. I never heard him complain about tiring, even though many of our trips were in excess of 1,000 miles and made in a 1941 Chevrolet.

On one of our trips, we had been working in Florida and were on our way back to Nashville for the Opry. In South Georgia we had a mechanical failure and it was impossible to make the trip back into Nashville for Saturday night. We checked into a hotel, with our banjos, and it was amazing the number of old-time tunes he knew. The weekend was pretty well spent with our playing the banjos.

He had a great tendency to call people by the wrong name, or to give them a nick-name. He called me Ernest. A couple of classics to me were, "Ernest, you play good in a band but you're not a bit funny, are you?" Meaning of course, I had no comedy routine. Another was, "You pick good in a band but you don't sing a lick, do you?" The comedy and singing remarks were true since I had devoted all my attention to playing the banjo. I suppose all these talents, the singing, comedy, and banjo playing combined, that Uncle Dave had, added to my admiration of him. But, for him to say he admired my banjo playing was as satisfying as "writing home for five and getting ten."

Uncle Dave Macon and Dorris on-stage

It will take a considerable amount of practice and time to accomplish playing the banjo. This probably applies to anything that requires coordination. My first playing dated back to when I was four or five years old. However, I do not feel that starting at an early age will make one a better banjo player than starting ten or fifteen years later. The effort you put forth will determine how quickly and smoothly you progress. As I have often said, don't try to learn too much at once; if you are a beginner, learn a small portion and do that over and over until you have accomplished it with ease. I am also of the opinion that everyone who learns to play will come up with some original sounds of his own.

It has been a great pleasure to me to hear the many fine banjo players who have started playing from my style, and, encouraging too, to hear their own ideas and talents added into their playing. It could probably be correctly stated that I was the first person to expose this style nationally. I would honestly like to say "Thank you" personally to all of you who have learned from my playing.

One of the greatest honors I have received comes from the people who, since about 1946, have referred to three-finger banjo picking as "Scruggs-Style."